Chariots Of The

C000302314

A tribute to the gallant men who trained with
secret amphibious duplex drive tanks on
Fritton Lake and achieved great success on
D-Day and in the battle to liberate Nazi-occupied
Europe during the Second World War

By

Robert B Jarvis

BSc (Hons), MSc (By Research)

2003

Published by The Heritage Workshop Centre

Published by The Heritage Workshop Centre,
80a High Street,
Lowestoft,
Suffolk,
NR32 1XN

This edition first published 2003

ISBN 1-904413-04-8

Acknowledgements

I am indebted to the following people without whom this book would not have been possible

Lord Somerleyton

Mr Basil Jarvis

Ms Carol Tuckwiller, The National D-Day Memorial Foundation, USA

Mr Charles Lemons, Curator, The Patton Museum of Armour, USA

Mr David Fletcher, The Tank Museum, Bovington

Mr David German, The Staffordshire Yeomanry Museum

Captain G E Locker, The Light Dragoons Museum

Mrs Jane Jarvis

Mr John Pearson

Major J S Knight, The Queen's Own Hussars Regimental Museum

Miss Liz Barnes

Group Captain Patrick Hennessey, MBE, RAF (Retired)

Mr Patrick Rushmere

Mr Ray Jones

Mr Robert Collis

Mr S J Sims

Mr Steve Cox, The Sherwood Rangers Yeomanry Museum

Ms Susan Green

Captain W M Henshall, The Royal Dragoons Museum

In Memoriam

Group Captain Patrick Hennessey MBE, RAF (Retired)
who sadly died while this book was being written

Contents

Foreword By The Author   **6**

1. Making Tanks Swim   **7**

2. The Duplex Drive Tank   **16**

3. Instructional Wing 'A' Fritton Lake   **33**

4. Preparing For D-Day   **57**

5. D-Day   **91**

6. Amphibious Operations After D-Day   **106**

     a. Breakout From The Bridgehead   **107**

     b. Operation 'Veritable'   **108**

     c. Operation 'Plunder' The Rhine Crossing   **110**

     d. The Crossing of The River Elbe   **117**

7. Appendix A   **119**

8. Bibliography   **125**

9. Terms and Abbreviations   **126**

10. Index   **127**

Foreword By The Author

Whilst writing my last book, *Fortress Lowestoft,* I became aware of the significant part played by Fritton Lake in the Second World War. During the latter part of the war this former duck decoy in Norfolk played host to troopers from the British, Canadian and American armoured formations that were to use one of Britain's most bizarre secret weapons.

Fritton Lake became Instructional Wing 'A' of the 79th Armoured Division and was responsible for carrying out initial training on the secret Amphibious Duplex Drive (DD) Tank. For this purpose a Squadron of Valentine tanks, converted to the DD role by the addition of a canvas 'flotation screen' and a primitive single propeller propulsion unit, were kept on concrete 'hard standings' in the trees beside the lake. These machines were to be used solely for training as it was hoped, although far from definite, that sufficient numbers of the Sherman DD would be ready in time for D-Day.

One of the many local rumours surrounding Fritton Lake is that one or more of these experimental Valentine DDs were lost during training and may still be sitting on the bottom of the lake, waiting to be found. While there were training accidents which led to a few of the amphibious tanks sinking in the lake, one resulting in the tragic drowning of a young trooper, all of these tanks were recovered soon afterwards, being dragged out by cables attached to a winch at the far end of the lake.

The DD tank had never before been used in battle and as such it had remained a closely guarded secret. It was hoped that the element of surprise would play a decisive factor in the invasion against the Germans, who would have no idea what was about to hit them as they watched a flotilla of what appeared to be small rubber boats slowly approach their beach.

It is reported that many of the German machine-gunners, expecting to be faced with lightly armed commandos, stood open-mouthed on top of their gun emplacements as the small rubber craft climbed out of the water, each in turn revealing a Sherman tank.

I hope this book will serve both as a tribute to the brave men who trained and fought in this most eccentric secret weapon and also to reveal a little more of the secret activities that took place in East Anglia during the Second World War.

Chapter One
Making Tanks Swim

A Valentine DD afloat. The extended driver's periscope can be seen rising above the screen at the bow. Notice the central hinge in the top rail of the floatation screen, a characteristic of the Valentine DD. Photograph courtesy of Mr John Pearson

Major General Sir Percy Hobart

Major General Sir Percy Cleghorn Stanley Hobart or 'Hobo' as he was affectionately known by his men, was a decorated First World War Royal Engineers officer and one of the most talented tank tacticians in the British Army, transferring to the Royal Tank Corps in 1923. Before the Second World War he created the world's first tracked tank Brigade and developed a new theory of mobile armoured warfare that found little favour with his superiors but was adopted enthusiastically by the new German Panzer commanders. In 1938 he was posted to Egypt where he trained the 7th Armoured Division, who went on to find fame as the Desert Rats.

As the Second World War drew near the clear-thinking and straight talking Hobart made many powerful enemies resistant to innovation, who wanted to perpetuate the horse cavalry with its distinction of class. By 1939 at the rank of Major General his career took a disastrous turn when he was placed on the retired list after falling foul of his superior officers. It was during a frustrating year spent serving as a Lance Corporal (and then area co-ordinator) in the Local Defence Volunteers that Hobart moved to Deddington before being recalled to active duty by Churchill in October 1940.

After his reinstatement Hobart raised and trained a new Armoured Division (11th Armoured Division, the Black Bulls) but before he could command them in action he was reassigned to raise the 79th Armoured Division. Its role was to devise and procure specialised armour to overcome the natural and man-made hazards likely to be encountered on the Normandy beaches. Hobart's 'funnies', as his swimming tanks, flame-throwers, minefield flails etc., were commonly known, were used extensively on D-Day and subsequently on crossings of the Rhine and the Elbe.

Some historians attribute the disparity between British and American casualties on D-Day to the decision by General Omar Bradley to use primarily dismounted engineers to overcome the beach obstacles on D-Day, while the 'funnies' of the 79th Armoured Division were able to execute a mounted breach of the German 'West Wall'. General Eisenhower later said that without them it was doubtful whether a bridgehead would ever have been established on D-Day.

Hobart retired from the Army in 1946 and became Lieutenant Governor and Secretary of the Royal Hospital, Chelsea in 1948, when it is thought he moved away from Deddington. He died in 1957.

Major General Sir Percy Hobart.
Imperial War Museum Photograph

The 79th Armoured Division

The 79th Armoured Division was formed as a normal armoured formation at Leeds in September 1942. By 1943 American opinion had hardened in favour of a direct blow against Germany through France and Belgium as the only certain method of ending the war. A direct assault on a fortified coast held by the enemy was a formidable task, the nature of which had been underlined by the alarming experiences of the disastrous amphibious raid on Dieppe in 1942.

At Dieppe tanks couldn't get off the beaches and the infantry, without adequate on-scene fire support, were slaughtered. Unless something was done to resolve this problem immediately there would never be a forced entry into France to oust the Germans and win the war.

Speed was essential in the penetration of the enemy defences and was even more vital in the subsequent build-up following the initial assault. In 1944 the problem became more serious, for the enemy defences (obstacles both above and below the tide-line, gun emplacements and minefields) increased by day as the Germans attempted to make good the shortfalls in the West Wall which had been disclosed by a recent survey. With every passing day the task of the attackers became more formidable.

The German defensive crust could only be penetrated by specially constructed armoured vehicles, but there would never be enough of this specialised armour to meet all the requirements, like landing craft it would always be in very short supply.

In 1942 there was simply not time to rebuild the entire allied Army or to improve vehicle and equipment with totally new designs to overcome the German countermeasures. There was just enough time however for a Division's worth of specialised vehicles to be adapted from existing machines that could act as spearheads to overcome the battlefield problems created by the Germans and then hope that this temporary relief would be just enough to allow a bridgehead to be established.

To lead such a Division the allies needed a man that not only understood combat engineering and tanks, but who could create an entire Armoured Division of them, with sapper devices to break through the defences being built by Field Marshall Erwin Rommel.

The Commander of the 79th Armoured Division, Major-General Hobart, was charged with the responsibility for the evolution, development, training and operational control of the specialised armour needed by the invading troops to land successfully in the face of enemy opposition.

The Division was composed of entire units with a single type of specialised vehicle to solve basically one battlefield problem type as outlined below.

Problem	Solution
Swimming Ashore	Landing craft/amphibious medium Duplex Drive (DD) tanks/amphibious personnel/vehicle carriers
Landmines	Flail medium tanks/rocket line charges
Soft sand/blue clay	Mat-laying medium tanks
Ditches	Fascine bundle dropping medium tanks/medium tanks with overhead ramps
Strong points	AVRE medium tanks with demolition guns/flame thrower medium tanks
Automatic weapons fire	Medium tank armoured personnel carriers
Night Assault	Canal Defence Light (CDL) medium tanks

With its specialist function the 79th Armoured Division was unique. It was the largest armoured formation in the 21st Army Group and while it never fought on its own, it was the only armoured formation whose units fought with every Brigade, Division and Corps in both the British and Canadian armies, in France and North-West Europe from June 1944 onwards. Commanders of all Divisions paid tribute to the value of the specialised equipment handled by the 79th.

Churchill Assault Vehicle Royal Engineers (AVRE) photographed where it now stands in France overlooking the site of the Normandy landings. The spigot mortar that replaced the main armament was capable of throwing a demolition charge a distance of up to 90 yards

As the nucleus of the 79th Armoured Division, Major-General Hobart had the 27th Armoured Brigade, which had been part of the Division since its formation in 1942, long before it was given its specialist role. The 27th Armoured Brigade was selected to man and operate the Duplex Drive (DD) tanks on which this book is focused. This required the Brigade to gain a mastery of the sea, to prepare itself for the beach assault against static enemy gun emplacements and then the advance inland as a normal armoured Brigade to take as much ground as possible. This formidable task was studied in great detail as far as the land operations were concerned, but for which no preparations could be made at sea as the DD tanks were not yet available.

To the 27th Armoured Brigade was added the Assault Brigades Royal Engineers. The 1st Assault Brigade Royal Engineers joined the Division in May 1943 and consisted of the 5th, 6th and 42nd Assault Regiments Royal Engineers. The Dieppe raid had shown the need for specially trained sappers equipped with modified armoured vehicles that allowed them to cross or carry out demolition of enemy defences while under fire. The Assault Vehicle Royal Engineers (AVRE) was a Churchill Mark IV with a spigot mortar in place of the main armament, which was capable of firing a demolition projectile a distance of about 90 yards. Additional modifications included fittings that allowed the AVRE to carry a fascine, or twenty feet long assault bridge. Either of these could be dropped by operating a control inside the tank without exposing the crew to enemy fire and provided a means of crossing ditches and rivers.

On the hull of the AVRE were racks for the carriage of explosive charges specially shaped for maximum effect against both concrete and steel armour plating. A frame of these charges could be carried in front of the AVRE and placed in position against an obstacle without the need to expose any of the crew. The AVRE could also push a 'Snake', a 4-inch iron tube filled with explosive that could be assembled in lengths of up to 400 feet. With a special head to prevent it digging into the ground, this could be pushed across an enemy minefield and then detonated, the blast supposedly detonating any mines either side of the Snake to a width of 16 feet.

An alternative to the AVRE was the 'Ark', also built on a Churchill IV chassis. The Ark was a de-turreted tank with runways over its own tracks and could be driven into a ditch or similar obstruction and, after lowering the ramps it carried would enable other tanks and vehicles to drive over it.

Other units of the 79th Armoured Division

In addition to the 27th Armoured Brigade and the Royal Engineers Assault Brigades a number of other units joined the Division, each charged with carrying out a specialist task. In the summer of 1943 the 35th Tank Brigade who had been trained to operate Canal Defence Light (CDL) tanks carrying armoured searchlights to illuminate the enemy's defences joined the Division. (The 35th Tank Brigade were replaced in this role by the 1st Tank Brigade, March 1944).

Originally the searchlight was installed in the Matilda tank in a special turret replacing the tank's 2-pdr gun. The operator, who sat in the other half of the turret, could control its elevation and direction by operating hand wheel controls. Light passed through a 2-inch wide slit covered by an armoured shutter that could be closed and opened by power causing a flicker effect that made aiming at the light difficult. Originally it was hoped to blind the enemy by making his eyes continually adapt to alternate light and darkness but this was found to be impracticable and the device was never used for its intended role in action. It was, however, used successfully to illuminate the river crossing operations that took place after D-Day.

In November 1943 the 30th Armoured Brigade joined the Division specifically for the task of destroying mines on the enemy beaches. A number of experiments had been carried out with every type of minesweeping roller; plain, spiked and jagged. They all had the same problem in that they were liable to bridge the mine by consolidating ground on either side of it, thereby preventing the roller from making contact with the mine.

To overcome this problem the Scorpion was devised. Originally this was a Matilda Tank with a box turret but no gun. Two booms projected in front of the tank carrying a drum or roller to which lengths of chain or wire rope were attached. The roller could be turned by an auxiliary engine mounted behind the turret that turned the drum via a shaft that ran along one of the booms. The booms were not adjustable for height but on level ground the chains ploughed the ground to a depth of three or four inches and detonated any mine that they struck. Flailing speed was slow, 1 – 1.5 miles per hour and the machines were only used singly, making a track about 8 – 9 feet wide.

Because every available tank gun was needed in the assault on D-Day, the 79th Armoured Division had to develop a mine-clearing tank that retained its main armament and so could function as a normal battle tank when not clearing mines. The end result was the Crab, a design that retained the roller and chains of the Scorpion, but with the drive to the roller supplied by the main engine. The tank gun was retained, allowing it to support other Crabs in the hazardous and dangerous task of sweeping when not flailing itself. Flailing speed was the same and the dust attracted hostile fire. German Teller mines could be detonated to a depth of up to 4 - 5 inches, each mine accounting for one chain. It is estimated that a Crab could explode up to 12 to 14 mines before having to redress the roller with new chains.

In addition to the various 'funnies' so far described, a number of Churchill VII tanks were adapted with the Crocodile Flame gun that had an effective range of up to 90 yards and which could be installed in place of the bow machine-gun. The tank towed a trailer with 400 gallons of fuel and nitrogen bottles, the latter providing the necessary propulsive power for the fuel. Under high pressure the gas was apt to leak, so it was therefore essential not to pressure up too soon before an action if effective flame fire was to be available. The original flame Regiment, 141st Royal Armoured Corps (the Buffs), was not part of the 79th Armoured Division but came under command in France when the armoured Brigade it belonged to found difficulty in arranging its operational deployment. It was later joined by the 1st Fife and Forfar Yeomanry and later the 7th Royal Tank Regiment.

Chapter Two

The Duplex Drive Tank

Valentine XI DD possibly photographed at Fritton Lake.
Photograph courtesy of Mr John Pearson

The General Motors diesel-powered Valentine was the first type of tank to be converted to the amphibious Duplex Drive (DD) role. The Valentine was one of the most widely produced of the British tanks (by early 1944 when production ceased 8,275 had been built) and in the desert campaigns they proved good fighting vehicles, although they were hampered by the 2-pdr armament and their lack of speed. After 1943 its value as a fighting tank declined and the type was used as the basis for a long string of special-purpose vehicles such as flame-thrower and DD tanks. A total of 650 Valentines were converted to the DD role.

There were three types of Valentine DD. The first was based on the Valentine MK V, which had a GMC 138 horsepower diesel engine (compared with the MK I's 135hp AEC 6 cylinder petrol engine). The main armament was a 2-pdr gun (40mm) and co-axial Besa machine gun. The turret was modified to accommodate an additional crewman. This gave them a considerable advantage over conventional Valentines, which only had space in the turret for the gunner and commander, forcing the commander to double as the loader and so reducing the fighting capability of the tank. The gun mantlet was also changed and the commander's hatch was re-positioned towards the rear of the turret.

The second Valentine DD was based on the MK IX and was an up-gunned version of the MK V, with a 6-pdr gun (57 mm) replacing the 2-pdr. To accommodate the bigger gun the co-axial machine gun and the provision for the loader had to be dropped, reducing the turret crew to two men, the commander doubling as the gun loader. A third type of Valentine DD, based on the MK XI was also produced, intended for use in the Far East.

At first it was thought the Valentine should be the main amphibious tank, but in 1944 it was decided that this role should be taken over by the Sherman M4, with the Valentine DDs retained for training tank crews in the skills needed to handle a 'swimming' tank.

The inventor of the DD tank, Mr Nicholas Straussler, who also designed the Straussler armoured car, was spurred into action following the British and Canadian disaster at Dieppe when landing craft were shown to be extremely vulnerable while unloading their tanks on the beach. He came up with a way of making a conventional tank swim, an ability that would enable the tanks to be launched further out to sea, reducing the risk to both tank and landing craft of being successfully targeted by shore batteries.

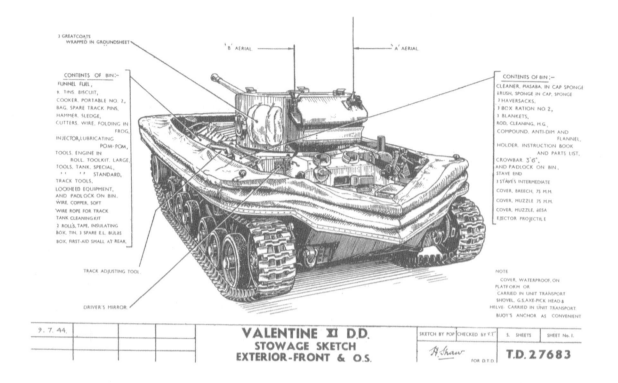

) GREATCOATS
WRAPPED IN GROUNDSHEET

'B' AERIAL

'A' AERIAL

CONTENTS OF BIN:-
FUNNEL FUEL,
9. TINS. BISCUIT,
COOKER. PORTABLE NO. 2,
BAG. SPARE TRACK PINS,
HAMMER. SLEDGE,
CUTTERS. WIRE. FOLDING IN
FROG,
INJECTOR,LUBRICATING
POM-POM,
TOOLS. ENGINE IN
ROLL. TOOLKIT. LARGE,
TOOLS. TANK. SPECIAL,
'' '' STANDARD,
TRACK TOOLS,
LOCKHEED EQUIPMENT,
AND PADLOCK ON BIN.
WIRE. COPPER. SOFT
'WIRE ROPE FOR TRACK
TANK CLEANING KIT
2 ROLLS. TAPE, INSULATING
BOX. TIN. 3 SPARE E.L. BULBS
BOX. FIRST-AID SMALL AT REAR.

CONTENTS OF BIN :-
CLEANER. PIASABA. IN CAP SPONGE
BRUSH. SPONGE IN CAP, SPONGE
3 HAVERSACKS,
3 BOX RATION NO 2,
3 BLANKETS,
ROD. CLEANING. H.G.
COMPOUND. ANTI-DIM AND
FLANNEL,
HOLDER. INSTRUCTION BOOK
AND PARTS LIST,
CROWBAR 3'6",
AND PADLOCK ON BIN,
STAVE END
3 STAVES INTERMEDIATE
COVER. BREECH. 75 M.M.
COVER. MUZZLE 75 M.M.
COVER. MUZZLE. BESA
EJECTOR PROJECTILE

TRACK ADJUSTING TOOL

DRIVER'S MIRROR

NOTE
COVER. WATERPROOF. ON
PLATFORM OR
CARRIED IN UNIT TRANSPORT
SHOVEL. G.S.AXE-PICK HEAD &
HELVE- CARRIED IN UNIT TRANSPORT
BUOY'S ANCHOR AS CONVENIENT

| 9. 7. 44. | | | | | | VALENTINE XI D.D. STOWAGE SKETCH EXTERIOR-FRONT & O.S. | SKETCH BY POP | CHECKED BY F.T. | S. SHEETS | SHEET No. 1. |
| | | | | | | | H. Shaw FOR D.T.D | T.D. 27683 | |

In order to make a tank swim he had first to overcome the problem of its lack of buoyancy. To do this Mr Straussler reinforced the track guards and attached a canvas screen to them that could be raised to displace sufficient water to allow the tank to float. This was reinforced by three horizontal rails and locked into place by vertical mechanical struts.

The screen was raised by air columns made of rubber tubes secured to the track guard at their base and inflated by a high-pressure airline that caused them to straighten, lifting the upper rail of the screen when inflated. The rubber air columns were of their natural black colour and some were full height while others only rose to the second horizontal support rail.

Flotation Screen

The flotation screen was constructed of three strips of tan canvas, the lower section being three sheets thick, the middle two sheets thick, and the top a single sheet thick. The canvas was sewn to metal strips, which were then attached to the support frames. The front section of screening had an additional canvas piece added on top and later vehicles added another at the stern. The additional height of the front section of the screen and the greater wave forces subjected meant that the bow struts were of a more elaborate design than the other support struts.

The Vickers Light Tank MK VII 'Tetrarch'. Armed with a 2-pdr (40mm) gun, this three-man tank was used in limited numbers with airborne troops. An experiment in 1941, shown in the top two images, was carried out using the Straussler flotation system to make the tetrarch capable of river crossings.

This pre-dates the use of the Valentine tank with this system

There were considerable differences in screen construction between tanks as they were converted quickly from existing vehicles and no two turned out exactly the same. There were also some differences between the British and American conversions.

Compressed air for the screen's rubber support columns was initially supplied from cylinders mounted on the rear deck of the Valentine DD and one or two similar cylinders were often mounted on the bow of the early (D-Day) Sherman DD tanks. The columns were inflated while the tank was still in the transport ship and there was said to have been sufficient air to supply the tank's needs

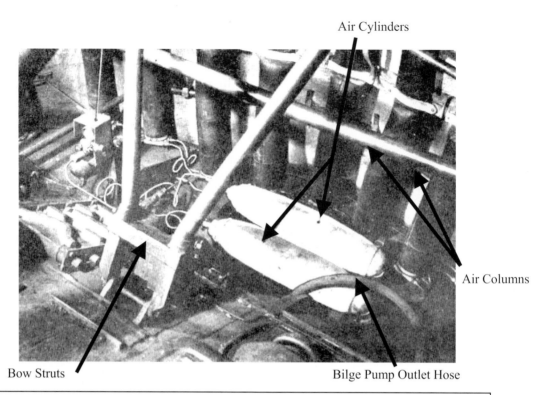

Air Cylinders

Air Columns

Bow Struts

Bilge Pump Outlet Hose

A photograph from the British Operator's manual for the Sherman DD showing the base of the bow support struts in the DD MK I. In photograph the pair of white compressed air cylinders are connected to the air columns by the thin metal tubing

even with minor leaks in the system, the cylinders being able to raise the screen twice before needing to be removed and recharged. Later DD tanks used their own air compressors, located in the engine compartment, for filling the support columns, with the compressed air cylinders retained as backups for the new air compressor.

On reaching the shore, the air in the columns was released by hydraulic pressure pressing upon air escape valves in the base of each column. At the same time, hydraulic pressure would also unlock the supporting metal struts (except the two turret struts in later vehicles which had to be physically unlocked by the crew). The header tank for hydraulic fluid was located next to the bow machine-gunner with the low-pressure hydraulic pump housed in the right rear corner of the fighting compartment. A number of rubber shock cords, surrounding the inside of the screen and connecting the screen's base flange to the top support rail, would help facilitate the rapid collapse of the screen.

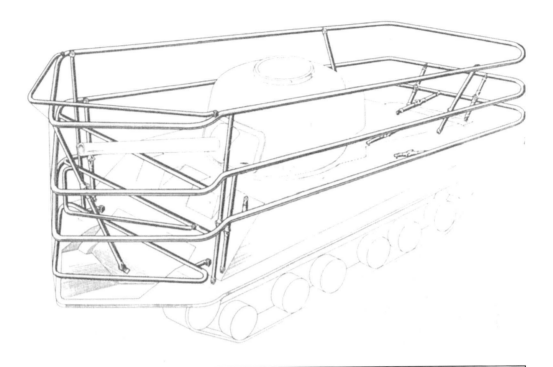

The support rail and strut arrangement in an early Sherman DD prototype. The later Sherman DD MK I was equipped with additional bow struts and the MK II was also fitted with a pair of turret struts and an extended rear screen to reduce the risk from swamping. Courtesy of the Royal Dragoons Museum

Once the screen was fully collapsed the turret could be traversed and the turret weapons used, while the propeller units would be lifted up to clear obstructions. The hull machine-gun remained blocked by the screen even when folded, however, and could not be fired until the screen was cut away by the crew. During the tank's swim ashore the bow machine-gun was usually removed and carried inside the tank, while the machine-gun's ball mount was waterproofed with a plug.

When afloat, the longer Sherman V displaced more water but floated higher than the Sherman III. Freeboard for the Sherman V was three to four feet, but the Sherman III only had two to three feet of canvas screen above the waves. Any appreciable swell could spill over the screen, especially during launching from the carrier vessel and the tank would sink like a stone if the electric and mechanical bilge pumps could not keep up with the incoming water.

This limited freeboard may have contributed to the loss of the American 741st Tank Battalion when they were launched in heavy seas too far away from the shore on D-Day. The tanks were carried off target by a strong rip tide, causing them to turn slightly to starboard to stay on course. This slight alteration presented the weaker side panels of their flotation screens to the crashing waves. Of the 29 Sherman DD tanks in this unit, only two made it ashore, most of the lost crews drowning in the water above their foundering craft. The other DD units were more successful as the Navy quickly realised the immensity of the problem and did not launch the tanks of the US 743rd, the Nottinghamshire Yeomanry and the 4/7th Royal Dragoon Guards until they were much closer to shore. The exception being the 13th/18th Royal Hussars, who were launched at 5,000 yards from the shore and swam successfully to the beach.

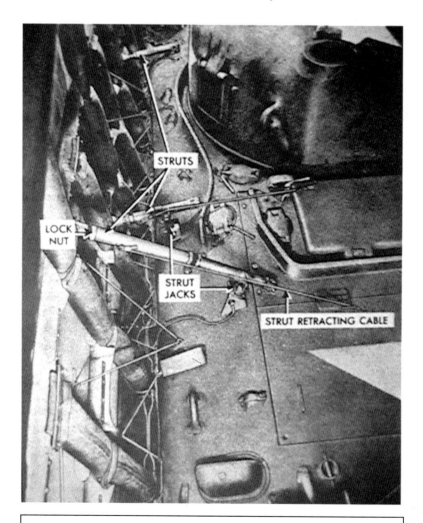

A detailed view of a support strut on an American Sherman DD.
Photograph taken from the operator's manual

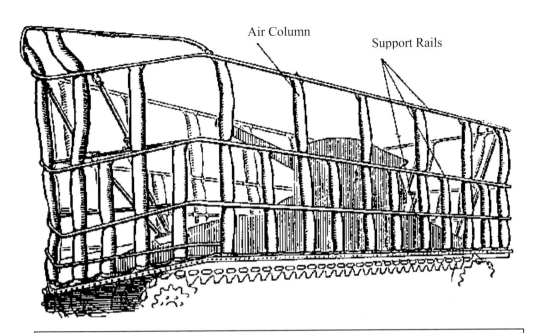

Air Column   Support Rails

Support rails, struts and air columns in the Sherman DD MK I. The additional bow struts and the lengthened rear struts can be seen in this drawing

A Sherman DD MK I of the Staffordshire Yeomanry photographed while training to cross the river Rhine. Courtesy of the Staffordshire Yeomanry Museum

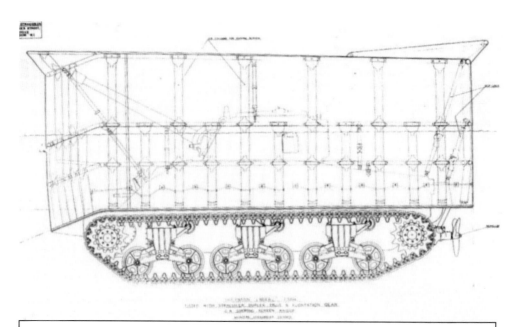

Blueprint of the Sherman DD MK II showing the arrangement of the rails, support struts and air columns. Note the extended rear screen section or 'apron' and the turret struts. Connecting directly on to the turret, these two struts had to be 'broken' by hand when the tank reached the shore to allow the gun to be traversed. Courtesy of the Royal Dragoons Museum

A Sherman DD MK II of the US Army undergoing training somewhere in the UK. Note the repair patches on the raised screen and also the twin propellers

Propulsion

Propulsion afloat for the Sherman DD was afforded by a pair of propellers (compared with the Valentine DD's single propeller) driven off the tank's gearbox that gave a sea speed of four knots. The actual Duplex Drive consisted of a pair of worm gears taking off from the idler/sprocket, turned by the moving track, bringing power to the twin 26-inch propellers.

The steering of the Valentine and Sherman DD tanks when afloat was accomplished by turning the propellers to left or right. At the rear of the tank is a horizontally mounted hydraulic piston to provide steering by a lever beside the driver's seat via a hydraulic oil line.

The hydraulic system was also used to lift the props from their drives for land travel in order to stop the blades striking the ground and, in later models hydraulic locking pins were employed to keep the propellers in the 'up' or 'drive' positions. In the earlier DD vehicles used during D-Day, the propellers would lift upwards and hence come out of drive when running astern.

A second method of steering was provided so that the commander, standing at the back of the turret, could steer by using a long wooden tiller behind the turret, connected to the propellers by a mechanical link. The commander operated his steering tiller while he stood outside of the vehicle on a small steel platform welded to the right rear of the turret. There was also a support column for him to hold on to while steering that was mounted directly on the roof behind his hatch and next to the platform. For navigation a 'Kelvin sphere' magnetic compass similar to those used in small boats was also provided, held in a bracket attached to the rear of the Sherman DD's turret, or positioned towards the rear of the deck on the Valentine DD. A second compass (eventually a gyro-compass) was sited in the driver's compartment.

The wooden tiller and compass were both removed by the commander before the tank hit the beach. The tiller connection entered the tank hull via a hole in the ventilator cover directly to the right rear of the turret. The connecting vertical link then joined to a long shaft that ran the length of the engine compartment, attaching to a cross-bar that connected to the two control links on the propeller drive units.

The driver generally only took over the steering as the vehicle approached the shore, when the commander entered the turret for protection from shore fire and could no longer steer by the tiller.

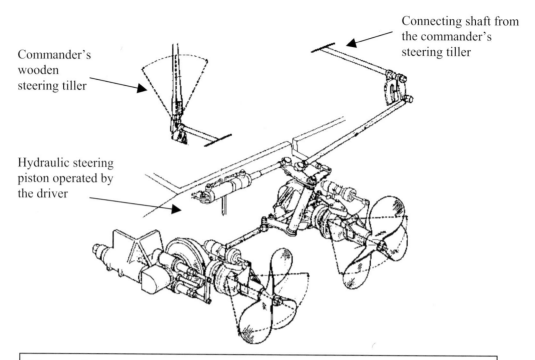

Connecting shaft from the commander's steering tiller

Commander's wooden steering tiller

Hydraulic steering piston operated by the driver

The steering arrangements of the Sherman DD. The connecting rod joining the commander's steering tiller to the 24-inch propellers runs the full length of the engine compartment but is shown broken by the thick line in this drawing

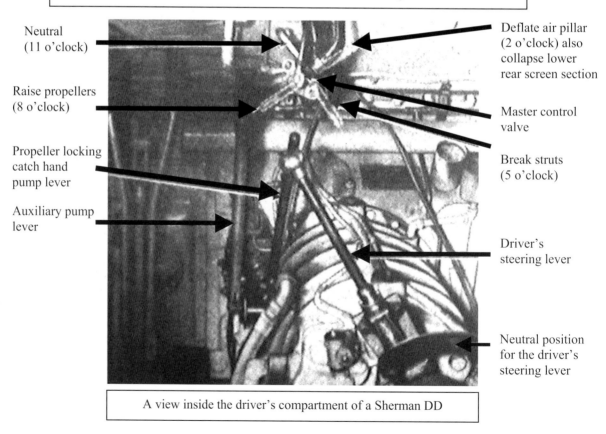

Neutral (11 o'clock)

Raise propellers (8 o'clock)

Propeller locking catch hand pump lever

Auxiliary pump lever

Deflate air pillar (2 o'clock) also collapse lower rear screen section

Master control valve

Break struts (5 o'clock)

Driver's steering lever

Neutral position for the driver's steering lever

A view inside the driver's compartment of a Sherman DD

Periscope

When water-bound and closed down inside their Sherman DD, the crew were able to see over the high flotation screen by using specially extended periscopes, one provided for the commander and one for the driver. The simple design incorporated a metal box of the same diameter as normal periscope bodies that would fit into a periscope holder used in the tank. An ocular tube with rubber eye-ring allowed viewing into the periscope and light was angled off a lower mirror up through the box periscope body. Another long cylindrical extension tube and accompanying optics then extended the view up and over the screen, ending in another angled mirror.

Focus could be adjusted at the ocular eye-ring but the field of view was very restricted and looking out of this small 'window' must have made for some very unwell crew when combined with the pitching and rolling of the tanks in the water.

Getting bearings for steering in a particular direction was assisted by rods attached to the top forward screen support hoop, which could be kept in alignment by looking through the periscope. The driver's extended periscope could be carried in the second periscope opening, located just forward of the driver's hatch.

A Valentine DD photographed at Gosport. Courtesy of Mr John Pearson

Sherman M4 DD

In November 1943 the first production meeting was held for the Sherman DD. Despite the known disadvantages of its petrol engine the urgency of production resulted in the first batch of Sherman DDs being converted from the Sherman MKV. While not as powerful as its German counterparts, the Sherman was prized for its versatility and rugged durability that made it the standard allied armoured fighting vehicle by 1943. One of dozens of variants, the M-4 A4 (called the Sherman V by the British) was the descendant of the widely successful M-4 A3, but unfortunately was an inferior substitute. It had identical armour protection and a 75mm gun, but its turret was awkwardly recreated and its engine was less powerful and offered a 100-mile range, making it less mobile and slower than its predecessor.

It would appear that the Americans were aware of the shortcomings of the A4 as they gave 7,167 of the 7,499 that rolled off the production line to Britain. British soldiers had a very disparaging name for the Sherman, the 'Tommy Cooker', so-called because of its unfortunate habit of catching fire and 'brewing up' when hit.

An American Army Sherman DD Mk II showing the rear screen could remain partially raised after hitting the beach to prevent swamping. The long vertical rod project from behind the right rear corner of the turret is the Commander's steering tiller, the shorter, thinner vertical rod projecting from the rear of the turret is the Commander's support column. An American Army photograph

The Duplex Drive Versions of the Sherman M-4 A4 were as follows

The Sherman III (twin General Motors 6-71 Diesel Engine) and V (Chrysler WC Multi-bank Gasoline 370hp Engine) DD, original conversions adding a screen erected by rubber tubing filled with air. Two propellers drove vehicle at 4 knots.

Sherman III and V DD Mk I, strengthened top rail.

Sherman III DD Mk II, Mk I with small improvements. In service after D-Day.

Sherman III and IIIAY DD Mk III, American conversion for Britain, with 76mm gun and HVS. In service late 1945.

British nomenclature for the Sherman DD tanks included the DD (Sherman III and V DD MK I) and DD I (Sherman III DD MK II). The latter referred to those vehicles modified or produced to the later standard with turret struts, self-locking struts and the extension of the rear screen panel to prevent swamping while climbing the enemy's shoreline. Those later vehicles fitted with power steering and an air compressor in the engine compartment became the DD II.

Public Record Office files containing monthly reports to Prime Minister Winston Churchill in 1944-45 give the following details on Sherman DD production.

Month	Number	Cumulative
Mar 1944	45	45
Apr 1944	175	221
May 1944	111	331
June 1944	96	427
July 1944	89	516
Aug 1944	75	591
Sept 1944	37	628
Oct 1944	27	655
Nov 1944	24	679
Dec 1944	14	693
Jan 1945	0	693
Feb 1945	0	693

(Acknowledgement to "The Sherman Firefly" by Mark Bill Hayward)

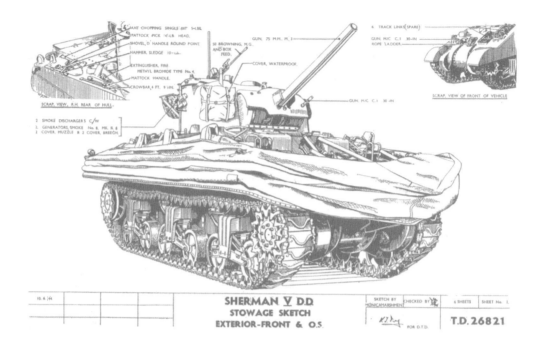

SHERMAN V D.D.
STOWAGE SKETCH
EXTERIOR-FRONT & O.S.

T.D. 26821

The types converted are not distinguished although it is reported that period photographs show examples of British converted M-4 A2 and M-4 A4 and probably M-4 A1, while the American conversions seemed to concentrate on the M-4 A1. The conversions continued post war with America converting some 76mm armed tanks for the British Army.

The number of DD tanks available after D-Day was generally very low. Reports in the war-time files note that, once used in normal combat with the DD gear stripped off, the tank would have to be virtually rebuilt to become DD capable again as often only the reinforced metal flange at the base of the flotation screen was left on the hull after the crews had cleared their vehicles for a more permanent land-based role.

Shown below are three sample weeks from various files in the WO 219/3350 series at PRO of unit holdings of the 21st Army Group, information supplied by the Sherman Firefly Book Web-Page.

13th January 1945

Unit	DD II	DD III	DD V	Total
HQ 79th AD	0	0	54	54
Total Units	0	0	54	54
Other holdings	1	18	33	52
Total all holdings	1	18	87	106

17th February 1945

Unit	DD II	DD III	DD V	Total
HQ 79th AD	0	0	58	58
Total Units	0	0	58	58
Other holdings	0	23	2	45
Total all holdings	0	23	80	103

13th March 1945

Unit	DD III	DD V	Total
*4th Armd Brgde	8	8	16
*33rd Armd Brgde	3	28	31
Total units	11	36	47
Other holdings	9	61	70
Total all holdings	20	87	107

* The 4th Armoured Brigade consisted of The Royal Scots Greys, 3rd/4th County of London Yeomanry, 44th RTR (DD Tanks) (11th Armoured Division).

** The 33rd Armoured Brigade came under command of the 79th Armoured Division for training between January and March 1945 and consisted of the 44th RTR (DD Tanks), the 1st East Riding Yeomanry and the 1st Northamptonshire Yeomanry.

There were reportedly no DD II listed either with units or in repair, or as other holdings at this time and none appear by the end of the war. On 16th June 16 DD III were held (none with units) and 83 DD V were held (none with units).

The Duplex Drive tank proved to be seaworthy up to seas of force 5 and its great advantage was that the swimming tank landed as a fully operational battle tank and not as an under-armoured and under-gunned machine whose buoyancy was only achieved at the cost of all its fighting qualities. For the first time assaulting infantry could count on immediate armour support, as or before they landed on hostile shores.

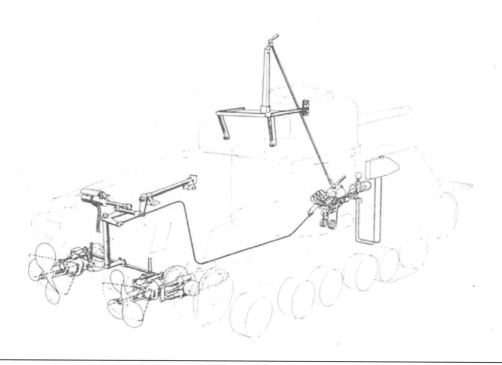

A proposed improvement in the hydraulic steering arrangements for the later Sherman DDs, showing provision for a Commander's steering handle attached directly to the driver's via a connection rod. It is not clear if this design was used. Courtesy of the Royal Dragoons Museum

Chapter Three

Instructional Wing 'A' Fritton Lake

A Valentine DD moored against the mock up landing craft ramp installed by the 79th Armoured Division at Fritton Lake in order to determine the best angle and depth of launch for a DD tank from a landing craft. Photograph by kind permission of The Tank Museum

The techniques to be employed by the 79th Armoured Division demanded a high standard of instruction and closely controlled development if unnecessary time-wasting experiments were to be avoided.

An instructional wing was established at Fritton Lake, manned by the best instructors available to pass on approved divisional methods and procedures to the troops who would be using the equipment concerned.

Instructional Wing 'A' at Fritton Lake was concerned with the freshwater training of the DD tank crews. The lake was surrounded by barbed wire and no unauthorised person was allowed in or out of the area. Even the farmers who worked the land overlooking the lake had to get permission from the army before being allowed on the fields in case the tanks were training on the water.

Valentines were the first type of tank to be modified for the DD role and had proved seaworthy and difficult targets to hit when afloat. However, little was known about launching them from landing craft and initial ideas on their employment were often based on unsatisfactory presentations and trials that had clouded the true potential of these weapons. To evaluate their worth the wooded area adjoining Fritton Lake was transformed. Here, escape drills were perfected and the method for launching from a landing craft ramp was tentatively established.

The initial freshwater speed trials on the first Sherman DD prototype unfortunately ended in the accidental sinking of a machine when it struck a submerged object, believed to be a tree trunk, in Fritton Lake. In order to gain data on ramp angle and the length of ramp required for a DD tank to successfully launch from a landing craft, the construction of a mock-up landing craft ramp leading into Fritton Lake was ordered.

It was absolutely critical to get the launch depth and ramp angle right. The Valentine DD floated in four feet of water, whereas the Sherman DD required a launch depth of at least eight feet at the end of the ramp. The maximum ramp angle for launching was established as 22° to avoid the vehicle plunging out of control down the ramp.

During the course of all these trials representatives of Mr Straussler's firm and Messrs Metro Cammel, the patent firm, were present and the first production meeting for the Sherman DD was held at Messrs Metro Cammel in November 1943.

A Valentine DD photographed at Fritton Lake during the initial Sherman DD fresh water trials. A Sherman DD with its open turret hatch clearly visible against the skyline is parked in the background to the rear of the staff car. A second Sherman DD with a crewman standing on the hull can be seen to the right of the Valentine's turret. Photograph courtesy of Mr John Pearson

In an interview recorded in April 1985 by Mr John Pearson, Mr Cyril Hutton, who was the assistant works manager at the Midland Works of Metro Cammel in Birmingham during the Second World War, revealed how he was one of the production team who spent some time at Fritton Lake during the initial freshwater trials of the Sherman DD.

Mr Hutton had been involved in strengthening the frame props and the track guard platform. His most important contribution to the Valentine DD was helping to change the design of the flotation screen top rail from one with four hinges to one with two. If the original design suffered a puncture in the air system it was possible for the affected end of the screen to fold down below the water level and sink the vehicle. Whereas in the modified design with only one pair of hinges, at least half of the 33 air tubes and two struts would have to be damaged for the same to occur.

The prototype Sherman M4A4 DD photographed afloat on Fritton Lake. The two men standing to the rear of the turret are presumed to be Mr Whatmough, Mr Cyril Hutton. The pipe-like object protruding above the flotation screen towards the front of the tank is the driver's periscope. Photograph by kind permission of The Tank Museum

Mr Hutton was later in charge of the design team that built the Sherman DD. The support rails in the Sherman's flotation screen had no hinges at all, although it was necessary later to add an extension to the rear screen panel to prevent a following wave swamping the tank. Mr Hutton also revealed that the bevel gears for the propeller drives were not of a high-tech design, but were the back axle gears from a Ford lorry.

The photograph of the Sherman DD afloat on Fritton was identified by Mr Hutton who recognised himself and Mr Straussler's assistant, Mr Whatmough, on the Sherman afloat on Fritton Lake. He was able to positively identify it as the first, but very brief test of a Sherman DD prototype on water and believed the photograph to have been taken in autumn 1943.

Although he was unaware that the photograph had been taken he remembered the event vividly. He said that he was on the tank to show complete confidence in his design as well as seeing at first hand how well it worked. The hull-sealing on this prototype Sherman M4A4 DD was not all it should have been and water had got into the high tension electrical system causing a serious misfire. Mr Hutton was low down on the hull at the front of the tank talking to the driver about this problem when he heard a tearing sound. He looked up and saw a tree trunk come through the screen at the front. For a brief instant he was able to look up through the water to the surface before he turned to pull the driver out. Both went underwater briefly but all on board were saved.

Because the engine had been running as the tank sunk it was completely destroyed, so when the tank was recovered a day or two later, the special DD equipment was removed and fitted to another Sherman. The decision was made that all Sherman DDs would be based on diesel engine version (M4A2) but it appears that this was not altogether possible due to supply problems.

Design work and improvements to the Sherman DD continued until after the war but Mr Hutton's last specific and dangerous involvement was in 1944. Following D-Day it was widely held in some official minds that the basic idea was a failure and it was thought that they could only be of use in none moving water and calm conditions. Various strengthening measures were undertaken and larger bilge pumps fitted. The rails and struts were strengthened with especial attention given to the locking mechanism and extra struts were added. An on board air compressor was fitted so that pressure in the system could be maintained.

The crew, along with Mr Whatmough, waited a fortnight at Studland Bay in Dorset for suitable weather and finally put to sea in a force 7 (40mph), with waves 9 to 15 feet high. The DD showed no signs of distress and swam around in these conditions for two hours. As a result of this it was decided to again use the DD.

The Sherman DD went on to see action at the crossing of the Rhine and other rivers in Germany, Holland and northern Italy. At Lake Bracciano in Italy the 3rd Hussars were introduced to the Valentine DD before handing them over to C Company of the 7th Hussars who continued to use them for training until they were issued with Sherman DDs for the famous crossing of the River Po.

The single propeller of the Valentine DD. Probably photographed while at Fritton Lake.
Photograph by kind permission of The Tank Museum

Mr Sims, who served as a Lance Corporal with the Royal Armoured Corps at Fritton Lake between 1943 and 1945, remembers the wartime activities at the Lake. The accommodation site for the non-commissioned members of the permanent staff was at Herringfleet Camp, which is used today by the local scouts. Originally the personnel at Fritton had to be back at camp by 23.00 hours, so their off-duty entertainment was usually limited a trip to the pub at nearby Lound. Facilities at the camp were sparse in the early days, although the fishing carried out by the permanent staff when off duty at the lake was apparently exceptionally good.

The permanent instructional and maintenance staff were at first housed in bell tents at the accommodation site beside Blocka Road, until four or five Nissen huts that constituted the permanent camp were built. The commissioned officers were housed in the nearby Herringfleet Hall. The NAAFI, a flat-roofed wooden structure, was not built until almost a year after the establishment of the camp.

The concrete posts in this photograph once supported the roof of the cookhouse at Fritton Lake. This is all that remains of the accommodation site, now part of the Herringfleet scout camp. Photograph courtesy of The Heritage Workshop Centre

Today the only surviving wartime features of the accommodation site are a few concrete pillars that once formed part of the cookhouse.

An area of woodland near the lake was cleared and it is here that the maintenance site was built. This consisted of the main workshop, a large Nissen hut resembling an aircraft hanger, where the tanks were serviced, a wooden hut where Mr Sims worked as an electrician along with a wireless technician and sometimes an additional electrician and a smaller wooden hut that served as an office for the officer in charge of the workshop.

A 'corduroy' road made from small trees laid side by side was constructed in the woods that run alongside the lake and allowed the tanks to travel from where they exited the water on the north side of the lake, back to the maintenance site and landing stage on the south bank.

Near the maintenance site the corduroy road was replaced with a concrete one, allowing the tanks to park when not engaged in training exercises. Located at the western end of this concrete road was the maintenance site, complete with inspection pits (one of which is now filled with water) and the main workshop.

Looking east along the concrete road from the maintenance site. The main workshop was to the right of this photograph. Author's photograph

The road ended abruptly in an area of concrete reinforced with lengths of railway track set in the shape of a cross. Here tanks would perform a skid turn and then drive towards the lake, descending the gently shelving sandy bank into the water and exiting on the far side of the lake. Later on, the Bailey bridge pontoons with their mock-up landing craft ramps were constructed a little further to the west. These were not installed at the lake until the early summer of 1943 and the First Regiment to be sent for training at the lake, the 13th/18th Royal Hussars, simply drove their tanks down the bank into the lake.

The corduroy road and maintenance site were hidden from view by camouflage netting, strung between trees suspended by ¼-inch thick steel wire, which is still present on many of the trees near Fritton Lake today. The camouflage netting served not only to hide the activities at the lake from the German air force, but also from the prying eyes of any curious locals who might have been in the vicinity.

The supporting wire for the camouflage net screen still hangs from many of the trees at the lake. Photograph courtesy of The Heritage Workshop Centre

Despite the presence of this camouflage screen, RAF air reconnaissance photographs taken in March 1944 show that the corduroy road, the accommodation and maintenance sites and even a number of tanks (both sitting on their hard standings and swimming in the lake) are clearly visible.

Training was almost always carried out during daytime, although night training was sometimes undertaken in preparation for potential night assaults. When afloat at night, a light was attached to the back of the DD tank's flotation screen to allow the tanks to keep formation, with a light positioned on the far bank of the lake to provide a landfall mark for the tanks to steer towards. As part of his work Mr Sims converted car sidelights into red, white and green signal lights to be positioned on an enemy beach by Combined Operations Pilotage Parties (COPPs) in the lead up to the main assault, which would be used as orientation markers to guide the approaching DD armour onto its target.

Looking north towards the lake from the skid turn area at the end of the concrete road. The route taken by the tanks is still clearly visible through the trees, the blue water of the lake indicating where the tanks would drive down the gently shelving sandy bank into the water

A tank crewman pictured wearing the Davis Submerged Escape Apparatus. Photographed on board a Landing Craft off Gosport. Imperial War Museum photograph H35172-35187

Further back from the lake than the workshop, up a slope, was located a water tank about twenty feet deep which was entered by climbing some steps and then descending a ladder inside. Here tank crews would learn how to use the Davis Submerged Escape Apparatus (DSEA) that was carried by every member of the tank's crew, to be used in the event of a sinking.

The DSEA consisted of a rubber bag attached to the chest that would be breathed into. The breathing bag contained a steel cylinder holding 56 litres of oxygen compressed to 1,200 atmospheres and a canister with a chemical for the absorption of the wearer's exhaled carbon dioxide. The control valve on the oxygen cylinder when opened admits oxygen to the breathing bag and charges it to a pressure equal to that of the surrounding water at whatever depth the apparatus is being used, allowing the wearer to breathe as a normal.

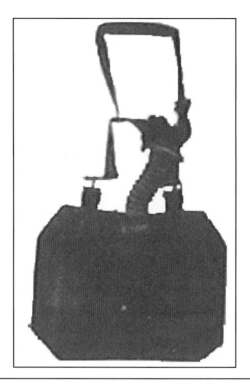

The Amphibious Tank Escape Apparatus (ATEA). Smaller and more compact than its predecessor the Davis Submerged Escape Apparatus (DSEA)

There were also two small steel capsules of oxygen with break-off necks in the breathing bag called 'Oxylets', as well as an emergency buoyancy bag in addition to the main breathing bag and a speed-retarding vane. This was an apron coiled on the underside of the breathing bag, its purpose being to retard the wearer's ascent to the surface when held in a horizontal position by the wearer.

The Amphibious Tank Apparatus (ATEA) later replaced the DSEA. The ATEA was a small version of the DSEA, sufficiently light and small to be worn continuously at the 'ready' by tank crews and to be able to pass through narrow hatches. It was charged initially with oxygen from cylinders carried on the tank landing craft but was also fitted with a single 'Oxylet'. In the heavy weather of D-Day many lives were saved by the ATEA.

Initially personnel trained with the escape apparatus in a water tower that had been built on a hill to the east of the maintenance site. First of all they had to get used to breathing while wearing the device, as the water pressure on the rubber bag when submerged gave great resistance to breathing and exhalations had to be forced. The coldness of the water also made the apparatus difficult to use as the mouthpiece often had to be held between chattering teeth. Once at the top of the water tank, the crews would descend the metal ladder into the water. Once at the bottom they would stand straight with legs crossed, partly inflate the bag by releasing some oxygen into it from the cylinder and, by pushing off with both feet, float to the surface while breathing from the bag.

Near this water tank was a small building that contained a concrete-lined brick pit in its centre, also about twenty feet deep, with a Valentine tank (minus it tracks and gun) placed at the bottom. Lights were installed so that the crews could see while they climbed down into the pit and into the Valentine tank. Here they would assume the positions they would be in while at sea in the Valentine, the commander and gunner in the turret, the driver in his seat, and would put on their escape apparatus. With the lights turned off personnel above ground would open valves emptying gallons of water into the pit to simulate a sinking. Once the pit was filled with water the lights inside the tank would be turned on and off once and the crew would begin to leave the tank in a predetermined order.

The permanent instructional and workshop staff of Instructional Wing A at Fritton would have to undergo escape training once a month. This may sound surprising but as Mr Sims relates, he often had to go out in a motor launch to tanks that signalled they were in trouble on the water and climb aboard.

Fritton Lake viewed from the air, 26th March 1944. The staff accommodation site was located at 'A', the officers mess (Herringfleet Hall) at 'B', the maintenance site at 'C', tank graveyard at 'D', concrete road and hard-standings at 'E', bank launching site at 'F', submerged escape training well at 'G', corduroy road at 'H' and Bailey bridge pontoon launching ramps at 'I'. The site of the Flying Fortress crash of 7th May 1944 is shown at 'J'

Before Mr Sims was sent to Fritton he witnessed the first three Valentine DDs ever to be tested on water at a large lake in the grounds of a country house at Narwood, near Swaffham, in the Spring and early summer of 1943. Here he saw the inventor of the DD tank, an elderly man called Nicholas Straussler, visit the lake to watch the progress of the trials and make modifications to the screen that needed extra support in the form of additional struts.

A few days after Mr Sims arrived at Fritton Lake, the only fatal accident of the war to occur at the instructional wing took place. A Valentine tank being driven by Trooper Leslie Charles Lloyd of the East Riding Yeomanry sank, resulting in the death of the young driver. Although Mr Sims didn't witness the sinking he was told that the tank was believed to have struck an underwater obstruction, rumoured to be one of the metal hawsers which had been stretched across the lake in the early years of the war to stop German seaplanes landing there. When the lake was taken over by the 79th Armoured Division metal hawsers were simply cut and allowed to sink into the lake, where they still remain.

Mr Ray Jones, a member of the East Riding Yeomanry training alongside Trooper Lloyd at the time, thinks that the Valentine being driven by Trooper Lloyd may have shipped water as it drove down the Bailey bridge ramp into the lake, a far more likely cause of this tragic sinking.

Mr Sims remembers watching the recovery of the tank. This was a very slow procedure, achieved by dragging the tank from the lake by cables passed round trees at the edge of the lake and connected to a winch.

The recovered vehicle was added to the graveyard of Valentines that was 'growing' in a depression immediately west of the end of the concrete road at the maintenance site. The tank graveyard eventually numbered about half a dozen Valentines and was the result both of accidental sinking, and swamping of the engine compartment when the flotation was dropped too early while the tank was trying to climb out of the lake.

To indicate the water level outside the tank, the driver was given a vital piece of apparatus in the form of a rubber tube resembling a condom that was attached to a hole in the front of the screen below water level. When the tank was afloat the tube would be filled with water. When climbing out of the water the tube would collapse as it came above the water level, indicating to the driver that he was sufficiently clear of the water to lower the canvas flotation screen.

A concrete support pillar from one of the maintenance site buildings.
Photograph courtesy of The Heritage Workshop Centre

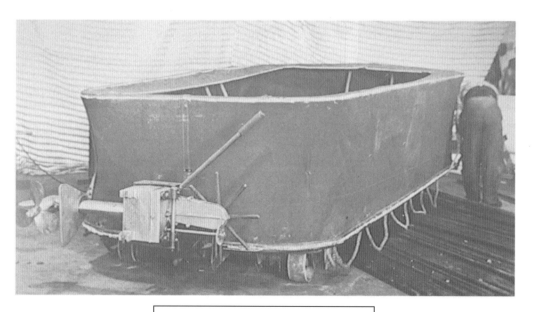

The DD Tender or Decoy

Unfortunately at Fritton the steep banks of the lake often resulted in the back of the tank still being under-water when the screen was dropped. As a result the tank would become swamped. To prevent this happening in the later Sherman DD tanks, an additional apron was attached to the back of the flotation screen, which would not be lowered when the rest of the screen was dropped upon hitting the beach.

As well as the more conventional (if that term can be applied to a 'swimming' tank) Valentine and Sherman DD tanks to be operated at Fritton, Mr Sims recalls once having to drive an example of the covertly named DD 'Tender' that appeared for just one day at the lake.

This flat-bottomed craft with the canvas screen of a Valentine DD was powered by what appeared to be a motor cycle engine and was in fact a decoy for the DD tank, designed to have the same outward appearance and speed as a DD tank afloat, but manned by a single crewman. The craft had an operational range of about one hour and could operate in conditions similar to the genuine DD tank. By late 1943 fifty of these craft had been ordered, half Sherman and half Valentine, probably with the intention to be used as a decoy during the D-Day landings.

A couple of weeks before D-Day General Eisenhower visited the lake to witness the American tank crews training with their Sherman DDs. A week before D-Day, around a hundred Sherman DDs arrived at the lake to be loaded with the ammo that had suddenly appeared, presumably brought to the lake by rail and unloaded at Saint Olaves railway station. After being armed the tanks then left for their embarkation ports. The tanks would be brought to and from the lake on tank transporters, each tank hidden from view by a tarpaulin.

Mr Sims, who had been in the vicinity of the NAAFI at the time, remembers another memorable event when two P47 Thunderbolts, *Lady Lorelei* and *Big Dick II,* operating from Holton (near Halesworth) collided and crashed into the lake on 8th April 1945. They were returning from a patrol and were practicing aerial combat tactics when they collided. He heard the explosion as they collided and afterwards saw smoke rising from the lake.

Other soldiers stationed at Fritton had witnessed the collision and glimpsed wreckage hissing and steaming as it sank. Patches of burning fuel were spreading rapidly on the surface and heat shimmering skywards blurred the far bank. The report written by Sergeant Alison of Oulton Broad Police Station, Lowestoft, on 9th April 1945, records that Sergeant Alison and PCs Mummery,

Houghton and Hopley went to Fritton Lake where the officer in charge of REME lent them a motor launch and a crew to make a search of the lake.

The discoloured water made it impossible to see below the surface, but a large quantity of oil was seen and they could smell high-octane fuel. Two rubber dinghies were recovered from the water and before returning to the shore the boat struck some submerged wreckage. Nine days after the crash divers from the Air Sea Rescue Service located and recovered the body of Lieutenant Judd. The body of the second pilot, Flight Officer Davis was not found until 7th May 1945, the day before VE Day.

The book 'Final Flights' by Ian McLachlan, gives an account of diving on the crash site in Fritton Lake, which began on 20th June 1971, with the permission of Lord Somerleyton. A torn-off tail plane and jettisoned canopy were among the first items to be found, twelve feet down in a sandy weed-free area about 70 yards off Lake Cottage. During the next five years further dives recovered other wreckage, including the smashed remains of a starboard wing now on display in the USAF Museum at Wright Patterson Air Force Base, Dayton, Ohio.

Another, potentially more catastrophic incident for the personnel at Fritton occurred at 08.15 hours on the morning of May 7th 1944 when a Flying Fortress from the 329 Bomb Squadron of the 100th Bomb Group (nicknamed 'The Bloody Hundredths') stationed at Thorpe Abbots, caught fire and crashed in woodland adjacent to Herringfleet Hall while en route for a raid on Berlin.

The aircraft was flying at 19,000 feet when some flares stored near the top turret caught fire and filled the cockpit and fuselage with smoke. The crew were unable to extinguish the fire and the aircraft went out of control after leaving the formation.

On impact one 500-lb bomb detonated, scattering the other seven and the wreckage of the aircraft over a wide area. Two of the 500-lb bombs were blown through the kitchen wall of Herringfleet Hall, demolishing a section of greenhouse and resulting in the death of five of the ten man crew, the remainder managing to bail out. Thankfully no casualties were caused on the ground.

Superintendent Clarke,

Two Thunderbolt planes – collision at Fritton on 8th April, 1945.

With reference to my report dated 9th April, 1945.
I beg to report that the wreckage of the two aircraft has been located in Fritton Lake, and the body of one pilot has been recovered.
The body recovered is that of 2nd Lieut. Russell P. JUDD, No. 0/552830.
Search for the body of the other pilot is being continued.

G. Allison,
Sergt. 27.

18.4.45

Police report on the recovery of the body of the pilot of the first aircraft on 18th April 1944

PHQ/WD.

Oulton Broad Station,
7th May, 1945.

Superintendent Clarke,

Two "Thunderbolt" planes – collision at Fritton, on 8th April, 1945.

With reference to my report dated 9th April, 1945.
I beg to report that the body of the second pilot, No. T/63496. Flying Officer Louis S. Davis, has now been recovered from Fritton Lake.

The wreckage of the two aircraft has now been recovered from the lake, with the exception of both engines which are apparently deeply imbedded in the mud.

G. Allison,
Sergt. 27.

18. May 45

Police report on the recovery of the body of the second pilot on 18th May 1944

Mr Sims and other soldiers rushed out with bayonets fixed as they were told at first that a German aircraft had come down. Later, when surviving airmen were found in the nearby countryside, the word spread that it was an American aircraft. Mr Sims remembers seeing one of the surviving crew wearing a torn flying suit who looked distressed. Following the crash Mr Sims and other personnel from the camp were sent out to look for the unexploded bombs that had landed in the wooded area opposite the camp, beside Herringfleet Hall.

The vicinity of the unexploded bombs to Blocka Road resulted in the road being closed to traffic for a while. The photograph below shows soldiers from Fritton engaged in the task of sweeping debris from the road under the watchful eye of British and USAAF officers.

Today the only public reminder of how close the war came to Fritton is a memorial stone erected by the Second Lord Somerleyton beside the entrance to Ashby church near Somerleyton, to the seven US airmen who were killed in the two crashes at Fritton.

Soldiers from Fritton Lake clearing debris from Blocka Road following the Fortress crash on 7th May 1944, courtesy of Mr R Collis and a similar view of Blocka Road today

"NEAR THIS PLACE ON MAY 7th 1944

1st LT. RALPH W. WRIGHT, LT. JACK W. RAPER, LT. RICHARD CURRAN,
LT. CARL A. HERRMANN, S/SGT RANDOLPH C. MOORE.

ALSO ON APRIL 8TH 1945

LT. RUSSEL P. JUDD, F/O LOUIS S. DAVIS
ALL OF THE USA 8TH ARMY AIR FORCE GAVE THEIR LIVES IN DEFENCE OF
THIS COUNTRY GREATER LOVE HATH NO MAN THAN THIS THAT A MAN LAY
DOWN HIS LIFE FOR HIS FRIENDS"

The memorial at Ashby Church erected by the second Lord Somerleyton.
Photograph courtesy of The Heritage Workshop Centre

An aerial photograph taken over Fritton Lake on 2nd March 1944 showing a line of DD tanks (probably American Army Sherman DD tanks) afloat on the lake 'A' and the exit site from the lake 'B'. The corduroy road is visible and can be seen running through the woods parallel to the lake

While the skills required to handle the DD tank afloat were being developed the land training of the Division went on without cessation. Units practiced their tasks from the moment that the DD tanks hit the enemy shore, through the fire-fight at the water's edge and the advance inland. It was obvious that survival depended on accurate shooting and since the tank's gun would not penetrate concrete the only solution was to unleash fire of such accuracy that the enemy gun could be knocked out where it protruded from its armoured emplacement. Constant training made this possible and when the Division moved down to Linney Head in Wales in the summer of 1943 a very high standard of individual training had been achieved.

Battle practices here formed the framework for a series of exercises covering lane gapping techniques and the necessary covering fire by day and by night when the CDL tanks were brought into the picture. Everyone took part, the DD tank Brigade, the Assault Engineers, the CDL tanks and Scorpions and for the first time the formation saw itself as a united Division and was able to realise how closely interdependent each part was on the rest. The drill was tested, changed and retried until something emerged that worked and could be adopted as standard procedure within the Division.

As soon as Linney Head was over another wing, Instructional Wing B, was started on the Solent at Stokes Bay. Within a week a camp had been assembled out of nothing and DD tanks and other equipment arrived for the sea training of the instructional staff that would man the wing. A flotilla of Landing Craft Tanks (LCT) was supplied by the Royal Navy and together tanks and landing craft set out to establish procedures for launching. On the first launch five tanks took two hours to become waterborne and two of these sank, yet within a week an LCT was discharging its seven tanks in just two minutes.

The training of the instructors was completed by the end of October and the first units of 27th Armoured Brigade came down to do their sea training. Valentines were the first tanks to be used, but as supplies became available these were changed for Shermans which had a more robust propeller drive, a better screen, and above all a better gun in the shape of the 75mm. Training at B Wing went on continuously and as soon as the 27th Armoured Brigade's training had been completed two Canadian Regiments, 1st Hussars (6th Canadian Armoured Regiment) and the Fort Garry Horse (10th Canadian Armoured Regiment) and three American tank battalions, 70th, 741st and 743rd Tank Battalions, arrived for training at the wing. The DD tank was the only piece of special armour to be used by the United States forces for their D-Day landings.

Chapter Four
Preparing For D-Day

A Valentine DD launching at sea

The 13th/18th Royal Hussars (Queen Mary's Own)

The 13th/18th Royal Hussars was the first Regiment to be sent to Fritton Lake for training with the amphibious DD tank. The men were told that the DD tanks were of a unique and 'top secret' design, and in them the Regiment was to swim ashore and lead the forthcoming assault against the occupied continent. Speculation among the rank and file was rife. Surprise was a vital factor and so the project was to be kept a complete secret. A grave responsibility, therefore, rested upon all ranks of the Regiment to avoid any talk as to the nature of the activities in which they were engaged. Security precautions were carefully and methodically organised and at this time it was only the senior officers who knew more than that, as the Divisional Commander put it, "the Regiment was to be put ashore in an entirely novel manner."

Everyone had to sign the Official Secrets Act and lectures were given to the men at frequent intervals. The facts of the Duplex Drive were not, at that time revealed, although it is doubtful whether anyone would have believed them. A canvas screen surrounding the tank does not sound very convincing as a means of flotation.

Initially the DD tank was to be the Valentine, but if production allowed, the battle model was to be the Sherman. Whether this would in fact be produced in sufficient numbers for the Regiment to use it on D-Day remained uncertain for several months to come.

Group Captain Patrick Hennessey MBE RAF (Retired) served as a Lance Corporal (Gunner Operator) with the 13th/18th Hussars during the Second World War. In November 1942 whilst stationed at Skipton in Yorkshire, he was told that the Regiment was to leave the 9th Armoured Division and become part of the newly formed 79th Armoured Division. He recalls the time when the commander of this new Division, Major General Hobart, was to inspect the Regiment. "The General passed down the line of tanks, his eyes glinting sternly behind his horn-rimmed spectacles. He was a tank man at heart and subscribed to the Tank Corps ethic that efficiency was more important than spit and polish. "Very nice", he said, "now start them up". The order was given and the crews leapt into their tanks, but to everyone's horror only seven tanks started. "It was clear that he was furious."

Here the Regiment was told, with the warning for the tightest security, that they had been selected to be among the first wave of the forthcoming assault on the shores of Europe. Many lessons had been learned from the disastrous landings at Dieppe. One of these had been that infantry landing on a beach without the support of tanks were doomed.

The role of the 13th/18th Hussars would therefore be to arrive in advance of the infantry and to enable them to do this they were to be equipped with tanks, which would swim individually through the sea. The idea that they were to swim their tanks across the water was at first difficult for the crews to understand, but eventually the principal of the technology involved was explained to them and they accepted that their tanks would displace sufficient water to float.

The New Year (1943) brought a major change to the Regiment in that their Covenanter tanks were taken from them and replaced with Valentines. This was to enable the crews to re-acquaint themselves with the Valentine, the tank in which they would be carrying out their DD training later that year.

Many of the Regiment had no previous experience with the Valentine tank, although some had trained on them in the early days of the war at Bovington, so the first training was to master its mechanism and maintenance. With this object in view, the Regiment received the first batch of 11 Valentines on 10th April, 1943 and immediately started to learn all about them. These were ordinary land tanks and had not been fitted with DD equipment.

They did not particularly lament the loss of the Covenanters. Although they were simple enough to drive and maintain, no one ever seriously thought they would go to war in them. Apart from that, they had one nasty characteristic. The turret lid of a Covenanter is one large sheet of metal which, to open is lifted, swung to the rear and secured in place with a spring clip. When the tank was in motion, especially over rough ground, it was possible for the lid to become disengaged from the spring clip when it would lurch forward into the closed position. Several tank commanders were injured this way and one unfortunate young officer was decapitated.

So the crews resumed their usual routine of individual and collective training on the Valentine, with road convoys, cross-country on the moors and live firing on the ranges at Warcop and Holmfirth, near Sheffield.

At the end of April the time came for the Regiment to leave Skipton. They were to move to a camp at Wickham Market, in Suffolk, conveniently situated for swimming in Fritton Lake, where they were to begin their training on DD tanks.

This special training was to be carried out under the supervision of the 79th Armoured Division, but in all other respects the Regiment remained under the 27th Armoured Brigade, now an independent Brigade with the 4th/7th Royal Dragoon Guards and the East Riding Yeomanry, under the command of Brigadier G E Prior-Palmer.

The Regiment's new camp was in a large area of fields a mile or so outside the village of Wickham Market. The Regiment de-trained at Woodbridge station and discovered how difficult it was to get all their tanks safely off the train. Eventually, they moved off by Troops and followed the guide to their new home. "Once again, we were in huts" recalled Mr Hennessey.

Because of the inherent danger associated with the amphibious role, an opportunity was presented to those who felt unable to take part in it to transfer to another unit. Several did so and they were replaced by new drafts, some coming from the infantry.

Eventually the time came for the Regiment to be introduced to the real world of amphibious tank operations. They moved out of Wickham Market a Squadron at a time, to spend two weeks training at Fritton Lake, a large inland lake surrounded by woods, originally a duck decoy. It was overlooked on one side by private houses and, owing to the very secret activities in which the troops were engaged, the unfortunate owners were subjected to considerable curtailment of their liberties.

The object of the training at the lake was to introduce the tank crews to their new and strange looking vehicles, to make them familiar with the associated equipment and to enable them to experience the unique sensation of being waterborne in a tank weighing several tons, kept afloat by only a flimsy canvas screen. They were taught the drills for raising and lowering the screen, the attachment and filling of the compressed air bottles, the operation of the propellers and the procedures for entering and leaving the water.

The training involved meticulous and detailed instruction in preparation, handling and navigation, both by day and by night. The keynote was safety first, since the Valentine tank, which was still being used for this particular training was at this time considered to be very unsafe afloat. Any neglect or omission in carrying out the simple drills might sink the ship with every possibility of loss of life.

On the first morning of their amphibious training, Mr Hennessey and his fellow troopers arrived to find a number of Valentine tanks lined up at the edge of the water. They looked much the same as their own Valentines, except that around the hull of each there was a folded layer of canvas. The instructors led the tank crews on a tour to inspect the tanks, pointing out the folded air-pillars, the metal struts, the propeller assemblies and showed them the stowage of the air bottles and how they were connected. They were detailed as crews, climbed aboard and watched with amazement as the air was turned on and the screens began to rise around each tank. Once erect, the screen stood about eight feet above the tank decking, with the result that apart from the tank commander, who stood on a platform erected at the back of the turret, the crew were blind.

Directing the driver over the intercom, Mr Hennessey's commander gave the order to start up and advance to the water's edge. Slowly they moved forward, entering the water, getting deeper and deeper until at last they could feel that the tank was afloat. By now, there was only some three feet of freeboard between the surface of the water and the top of the screen.

Standing on his platform and just able to see over the screen, the tank commander steered the tank by passing orders to the driver who held the steering tiller which was linked to the propeller. As Mr Hennessey recalls, this first encounter with the world of swimming tanks was fairly uneventful: "We cruised around the calm water of the lake for about 20 minutes on that first sortie so that we could get used to the motion of the tank afloat and savour the experience of being waterborne. Nautical jargon quickly sprang up in conversation and such expressions as 'port your helm' and 'coming alongside' soon came naturally to everybody."

"As we neared the beach, we felt the tracks find the sand and slowly we emerged from the water like some monster climbing back on to the land. When the hull was clear of the water the deflation switch was pushed, the metal struts broken and, with a hissing of escaping air the screen collapsed and once more we were a dry-shod tank."

During that time at Yarmouth the men of the 13th/18th worked with the DD tanks until they were fully conversant with all their aspects and became quite adept at launching into the water. They learned to navigate by sighting a landmark on the far bank and making that the steering point, they then mastered the complicated procedure for coming ashore. They discovered how to recharge and change the air bottles and how to operate the bilge pumps, which had thoughtfully been fitted. Here too they were introduced to many other facets of amphibious operations, including the waterproofing of vehicles that would have to wade through shallow water and they had their first experience of using Bostick, that black, sticky substance which was used to keep water out of vital parts of vehicles whilst they were temporarily submerged and several tins of this very smelly material were used at Fritton.

The whole Regiment was involved in this training, which was carried out in two parts, 'A' and 'B' Squadrons first for a fortnight, followed by 'C' and HQ Squadrons. The Regiment was comfortably billeted in Great Yarmouth and, on the whole, the training went well. There were no fatal accidents and nothing occurred to upset the crew's confidence in the Valentine DD, even though it was only an experimental model and had many imperfections.

Mr Hennessey recalls one incident, which will not easily be forgotten. It occurred during a night exercise that the Brigadier attended. "He selected a particular tank from which to watch proceedings. It had been stressed clearly and often during training that it was very important that fuel tanks be kept filled. It was, therefore, somewhat unlucky that the Brigadier should have chosen to travel in a Valentine which suddenly came to a gentle standstill in the middle of the lake with an empty fuel tank. The atmosphere was somewhat unnerving at the best of times in the blackout, with nothing but a tiny pilot light and a craft whose response to the helm was rather unpredictable. The chances of collision were odds on and would almost certainly have resulted in the sinking of both craft."

"With no engine, the tank was quite incapable of movement of any sort. Thus the scene in the tank and the feelings of the unfortunate subaltern in command can be imagined. To make matters worse, the motor rescue launch failed to start, and the Brigadier finally had to be taken off in a rowing boat, manned by four soldiers who had never handled an oar before. The future prospects for this officer did not look good, but the Brigadier knew that even the best young officers make mistakes and all was forgiven, but not before the Brigadier had expressed his views on the oversight in no unmeasured terms."

On completion of their initial training the crews returned to Wickham Market having had their first taste of their new amphibious role and feeling quite excited about it. Before long, however, they were on the move again, this time to the Royal Navy's Submarine School at Gosport. It was realised all too readily that the amphibious tank was a delicate craft when afloat and could all too easily become a steel coffin for its crew should it sink. As a safety measure, one which saved countless lives during both training and the D-Day landings, the crews of the amphibious DD tanks were to be issued with underwater escape apparatus, which the Navy would teach them how to use. The submarine service was supplied with a fairly bulky piece of equipment known as the Davis Submerged Escape Apparatus (DSEA), which had proved very effective from their point of view. However, because of the small entrance hatches on tanks, the DSEA would be unsuitable for the tank crew's purposes. A new and more compact piece of equipment, the Amphibious Tank Escape Apparatus (ATEA), was eventually devised for them.

Although a concrete well was installed at Fritton Lake by the summer of 1943, complete with the hull of a Valentine tank for submerged escape training, this training was initially carried out under the supervision of the Royal Navy's experts at Gosport.

Mr Hennessey recalls his experience of submerged escape training: "We started with a comprehensive description of the apparatus and a warning of the dangers of surfacing too quickly from the deep. Then, each of us was fitted with a kit and learned how to breathe with nose-clip and mouthpiece in place. We rehearsed, again and again, the procedure for surfacing drills. The climax of the short course came with an exercise which required us to put all this information into practice."

"We were led to an area where there was a large pit, lined with concrete, some 30 feet deep. Leading to the bottom of the pit was an iron ladder and on the floor of the pit stood a Valentine tank. Wearing only denim overalls and gym shoes, with escape apparatus strapped to our chests, we climbed down the ladder and into the tank, taking up our normal crew positions. When we were in place, a sluice gate was opened and water began to gush into the pit. We had to sit calmly in the tank as the level of water rose and only when it had reached chest height were we permitted to apply the mouth-piece and nose-clip."

"Thereafter, we sat still, breathing through the apparatus as the water rose far above our heads. When the pit was full we were given the signal, one by one, to leave the tank and rise to the surface 40 feet above, controlling the ascent by means of a valve at the side of the bag strapped to the chest."

"This was an experience that it was not easy to forget. It called for more than a little self control to remain seated in the tank under the weight of tons of water until permitted to surface, but having reached the top and climbed out there was a feeling of well-being and great elation which, it was explained to us, was caused by the fact that we were oxygen drunk through having spent some time breathing pure oxygen. The theory of this training was that if a DD tank should sink, there should be no panic. The crew had only to remain in their seats, don their escape apparatus, wait calmly till the tank had settled on the sea-bed and then come to the surface as we had been taught."

This was all very well in theory, but many of the crews had grave doubts. Nobody could guarantee that a tank would sink the right way up. Panic was not far off, even in the controlled discipline of the training well and although the idea was to give those involved confidence in the escape equipment, it also caused them to realise rather more clearly what it was they were being asked to do. Just before the 13th/18th left the Submarine School at Gosport, the Chief Petty Officer said to Charlie Rattle, "Rather than you me, mate!"

On their return to Wickham Market they learned that the Regiment was to be re-equipped yet again. This time their Valentines were to go, in their place they were to be issued the American Sherman M4 Tank. This was great news. The Sherman had proved itself in battle in the desert campaign. It was bigger, faster, better armoured than the Valentine and had a bigger gun. However, at the time it was still no match for the German tanks, a fact that the men of 13th/18th were happily oblivious to as they prepared the Valentines for hand over.

In May the Regiment received the first batch of Shermans and came on to a new establishment. This involved an increase in strength and a draft of about one hundred and fifty was received shortly after from the 104th Regiment Royal Armoured Corps. The Sherman was a new proposition for the Regiment, and a pleasant change from any tank with which they had previously been equipped.

When the first consignment of Shermans arrived at Woodbridge, a detachment of drivers and commanders was sent to collect them. The rest of the Regiment were standing on the tank park when the first of the Shermans arrived. Upon climbing aboard to inspect their new tanks the crews were pleasantly surprised to find the turret spacious and painted in a clean white finish, a great improvement on the dingy yellowing silver décor of the Valentine's cramped fighting compartment. There was plenty of room for the turret crew of three. The 75mm gun was twice the size of the Valentine's 2-pdr and, co-axially mounted was a 0.3-inch Browning machine-gun. On the turret hatch was a 0.5-inch Browning. The driver's compartment was also more spacious and next to him was a position for an assistant driver in front of whom was mounted yet another 0.3-inch Browning machine-gun. The tanks of the 13th/18th Royal Hussars now carried a crew of five.

The gunners in particular needed some element of retraining, as all of these weapons were new to the crews. The drivers also needed some revision and a number went off to Bovington for a specialised Sherman driving course. Within the large turret was the breech of the 75mm gun and the gun shield, though the crews found they could live much more comfortably, if more dangerously, if the shield was removed altogether. The gunner now sat on the right of the gun and controlled the elevation and depression of it by turning a wheel with his left hand, while his right hand controlled the spade grip of the powered traverse. The triggers were controlled through solenoids by foot pedals. His gun sight was combined with a periscope, which gave him a much wider field of view. The radio operator sat on the left of the gun, his radio controls at the rear of the turret and he had ample room to load the 75mm and to tend the Browning. The tank commander was free to concentrate on his main job of directing the operation tank, something he would have found much more restricting in the cramped conditions of the Valentine turret.

The local training areas were excellent and at Orford Ness there was a large-scale battle practice range. Training followed conventional lines. Squadron followed troop training, until the Regiment was ready for exercise 'Thet', which was due to take place at the end of July. The exercise opened with a review on Hollesley Heath, just outside Woodbridge. The entire Brigade was drawn up in open order with tanks in front, 'B' vehicles (supply and transport vehicles) behind and, on the flanks, the various services, including the Field Ambulance, REME Workshops, and RASC Company. After the review the Brigade moved off to the Newmarket area some fifty miles away, where for the whole seven days they were kept hard at work. The exercise finished with a set piece attack on Frog Hill, a well-known feature of the Thetford area. As a result of this training the Regiment gained the greatest confidence in their new tanks, which had behaved admirably.

On 20th August the Regiment moved to Linney Head for annual firing practice in South Wales. In preparation for their DD role a special and amusing firing practice was organised, each Squadron in turn lining up along the high water line and pumping their entire load of ammunition into the cliffs. This gave everyone a most spectacular demonstration of firepower and proved very encouraging for D-Day.

The return to Wickham Market was organised by the Warrant Officers and NCOs, the officers taking themselves off to London for 48 hours leave. This latter excursion was lightly given the codename 'Exercise Enigma' and was officially tempered with a visit to the Department of tank Design at Egham. At Wickham Market, where the Regiment was under canvas, there was little for the men to do in their leisure moments. They would go to Woodbridge and sometimes to Ipswich, but neither place could really offer what they liked in terms of entertainment. The officers were able to get some good shooting in at Orford Ness, which was well stocked with a variety of game.

On return to Wickham Market on 14th November the Regiment took part in a series of exercises known as 'Hedgehog'. These were set piece attacks against a dummy 'West Wall' and all arms took part. Infantry were supplied from the 158th Infantry Brigade, every sort of specialised armour was represented, including flails, AVREs and Crocodiles.

Before setting off for Gosport to do DD training in the sea, the Regiment carried out one more tactical exercise known as 'Alde', on 12th December. At this time a change in the tactical set up of the Regiment was made. Instead of all three Squadrons being amphibious, only two were required for this role. The third, with RHQ, was to land later and therefore would be trained in wading in six foot of water from LCTs. Thus it was that 'A' and 'B' Squadrons and RHQ proceeded to Gosport on 18th December, whilst 'C' and HQ Squadrons went to Hoddom Castle in Dumfriesshire.

The training at Gosport was hard work and gave little time or no break for Christmas. Work went on at all hours of the day and night in order to catch the tide. Twice in each 24-hour period the tanks would embark at Stokes Bay, cross the Solent and launch into Osborne Bay, Isle of Wight. This form of DD training was very different from anything experienced up to date. Although lucky with the weather, it soon became apparent that the tides and currents were very important factors in the way tanks handled at sea. These exercises were largely experimental and were watched by both British and American naval officers, who were concerned in the planning of the assault.

Captain Neave, the Adjutant, recalls in the Regimental history: "I can remember one bleak morning at dawn in a launch with General Omar Bradley (Commander of US Forces in North West Europe 1944-1945) and Vice-Admiral Sir Philip Vian (Commander of the Naval Forces at the assault on Normandy). Neither had any breakfast and the exercise was not going too well. Major-General Hobart was also there and the air was pretty tense and filled with acrimonious comment. But I kept in the background, hoping that nothing serious would happen and trusting that we were not really so bad as we seemed to be on this occasion."

This training was excellent and, although at this time it was still tied down to the dogmatic teaching of the school, the Regiment was gaining the experience, which was to enable it to develop its own ideas on arriving at Fort George on the Moray Firth. In Scotland their training became much more intense and the waves and storms on the Moray Firth paid dividends. At the start of their sea training the drivers were issued with extended periscopes, but they were so un-wieldly and restricted in their field of view that they discarded them.

Valentine DDs of the 13th/18th Royal Hussars during training on the Moray Firth. The gun turrets on these tanks are all facing backwards to allow the flotation screen to be elevated. Note the vertical exhaust pipes and lifebuoys carried by each tank. Interestingly, the tank in the foreground appears to be equipped with the 2-pdr gun, while the two tanks immediately behind are armed with the later 6-pdr. The commander's magnetic compass is highlighted with an arrow on the top right tank

On 1st January 1944 the whole Regiment concentrated at Hoddom Castle (the officers discovering that a castle is not the most cosy of places to stay during winter) and on 26th January the Regiment moved to Fort George, the peacetime depot of the Seaforth Highlanders, set on the beaches of the Moray Firth. Although greatly overcrowded it was an excellent barracks.

At Fort George, concrete hards had been built that ran down to the water's edge and landing jetties had been erected.

Mr Hennessey recalls his first encounter with the LCTs: "They had tall flat bows and were heading straight for us, they ran right up to the concrete and stopped. The flat bows lowered to form ramps leading up to an open space within the hulls of the ships. These were known as tank decks. This was our introduction to the Landing Craft Tank (TLC) and the naval officers and seamen who crewed them. In the following months we were to get to know them very well, because they were the ones who would take us to war."

Each LCT took five tanks and once the crews had mastered the technique of loading them to the satisfaction of both the LCT Skipper and the Squadron Commander, the TLCs raised their ramps and backed away from the shore with their precious cargo on board. "After a while our LCT hove to about 300 yards from the shore. We inflated the screens, the ramp was lowered and one by one we drove off, down the ramp into the water. The big difference this time was that it was not the calm waters of Fritton Lake into which we launched, but the waves of the Moray Firth. There was a difference and we felt it. Nevertheless, we all got ashore safely, drove back to the hards where the LCTs came to meet us and we repeated the exercise, again and again, each time the distance from launch to shore was increased."

The set-up for the organisation of combined training and rehearsals was on a large scale. The Regiment was under the command of the 3rd Division (Major-General T Rennie, killed in action in Normandy) and was to remain so for the assault on Normandy. The remainder of the troops in this Division were all located in the Inverness area. In addition to the three infantry Brigades, there were innumerable sappers, gunners, commandos and various specialised units, all of which were involved in some particular aspect of the assault.

The Royal Navy also had a force equivalent in size and diversity, known as Force 'S', which was distributed all around the Moray Firth and at Invergordon, and was destined to transport the Regiment across the Channel and put them on the beaches.

March 1944 resulted in a particularly unfortunate accident. The DD tanks were launched in the Moray Firth early one morning. The wind was rising at the time and when the tanks were half way inshore, a severe snowstorm broke. The sea became very rough and two tanks of 'A' Squadron were swamped and sunk. Lieutenant Denny and the crews were picked up, except for Corporal Underhay, who was drowned. This was the first and only fatal casualty suffered by the Regiment during DD training.

In all the Regiment lost five tanks during this period of training and were remarkably lucky not to have incurred further casualties. These losses were due to three main causes. Firstly, no one really knew the capabilities of the DD tank in a rough sea and it was obvious that the sea might not be as calm as could be wished on D-Day, as, indeed, it was not. Experiments, however, had to be carried out to find an answer and considerable risk had to be incurred in doing so. Secondly, even in a comparatively calm sea in which the tanks could navigate successfully when safely launched, the actual process of launching was dangerous. The tank drove down the launching ramp from the LCT on its tracks and then, when in the water, had to engage its propellers. There was, therefore, a few seconds delay before the tank started to move in the water and could get clear of the ramp. This was the danger period if the waves were at all large.

The tank was liable to be washed back onto the ramp and tear a hole in the canvas, which might result in the tank sinking in a few seconds. The third cause of loss was the fact that, once in the water, the tank could not be got out again until it reached land. It was not possible to drive it back into the LCT and, owing to the time taken for the swim in, it was quite possible for changes in the weather to take place between the time of launching and reaching the land. This actually happened on several occasions, when suddenly squalls blew up and disastrous results were only narrowly averted.

After each exercise a conference would be held at Inverness, attended by all officers and run jointly by the Army and Navy, where all problems and lessons would be thrashed out with little or no respect for personal feelings. These were gruelling days of trial and error.

From Scotland the Regiment returned to East Anglia, where they exercised in the area of Orford Ness and then to Wales for firing practice on the ranges at Castle Martin. Here they carried out manoeuvres with the flail tanks of the Westminster Dragoons in co-operation with the infantry and watched the CDL tanks working. Christmas 1943 was spent at Gosport, in Fort Monkton, the former home of the Royal Marines.

On the 5th February 1944 General Sir Bernard Montgomery arrived at Fort George to visit all troops in that neighbourhood who were to take part in the assault. It was a particularly cold day, the parade numbered some 3,000, and the Regiment, which was the senior in the Fort, was made responsible for all arrangements.

When the Regiment left Fort George on 16th April 1944, it was for the south of England for the invasion itself. To start with the Regiment was located in three different places. 'A' and 'B' Squadrons (equipped with DD tanks) were at Gosport, but still without their new Sherman DDs, owing to delay in production. 'C' Squadron and RHQ were at Petworth Park in Sussex and the various administration echelons were at Aldershot.

In May 1944 after a short period in the attractive village of Petworth, the Regiment returned to Gosport, and were sent in batches on seven days leave as Mr Hennessey recalls: "It was embarkation leave, although nobody said so at the time, few of us thought otherwise. When the leave cycle was finished, we found in the last week of May that we were strictly confined to barracks. We were virtually sealed in with no mail or telephone calls allowed. We shared our camp with two Canadian Regiments, the 1st Canadian Hussars and the Fort Garry Horse. Both of these Regiments had also been trained on DD tanks. The Canadians had a reputation for being wild and it was rumoured that the Fort Garry Horse had shot their cook because they were dissatisfied with the quality of their food. We chose to believe this but I doubt if it was true."

At Gosport 'A' and 'B' Squadrons worked intensively at conversion courses on the Sherman tank, but were still without many of the actual tanks they would take over the Channel. When these did arrive and some did not do so until the last minute there were many teething troubles to be overcome. These technical difficulties required continual reference to Headquarters Southern command and the War Office. But, owing to great congestion on the telephone lines, communication was virtually impossible.

The solution was found when Colonel Raikes of the Fighting Vehicle Inspectorate, War Office and Major Brown of the Directorate of Tank Design, arrived at Gosport to give assistance. Quickly realising the very real troubles with which the Squadrons were confronted, Colonel Raikes decided to live with them until D-Day and his authority very soon made itself felt, Squadron fitter staffs working cheerfully and unceasingly through all hours of the day and night.

Activity at Petworth was equally intense with water-proofing of vehicles, the storing of innumerable loads of new equipment, and a seemingly endless amount of paper work. Landing and loading tables had to be worked out, planning notes and directives issued, while 'top secret' orders for which special precautions had to be taken poured in.

The Regiment took part in one more final exercise, 'Fabius', on 29th April 1944. This exercise was designed to iron out the difficult problem of marshalling and loading. 'A' and 'B' Squadrons had an easy time, since they were already on the hards at Gosport and only had to load themselves into their LCTs on the spot. 'C' and RHQ Squadrons, on the other hand, had to move from Petworth to marshalling camps near Portsmouth and endure the full inconvenience and trials inherent in the process of marshalling and embarkation.

A marshalling area is defined in military text books as 'an area normally five to ten miles from the coast to which personnel and vehicles are moved in readiness for embarkation and where units are marshalled into ship and craft loads'. Marshalling is a vastly complicated procedure. The technique had been evolved in the many amphibious operations that had already taken place in the invasions of North Africa, Sicily and Italy.

But the invasion of Northern Europe was on a much larger and more complicated scale then any previously undertaken.

For the Regiment Fabius involved a cruise in the Channel under an immense air umbrella, followed by a landing just west of Littlehampton. It finished with a manoeuvre on the South Downs before the Regiment returned, once again, to Petworth. It provided a most valuable dress rehearsal for the final embarkation.

There was now just one month before D-Day and the work of final preparation continued with feverish activity interspersed with periods of tedious waiting. On 1st June the Regiment received orders to move to its marshalling area at Waterlooville, near Portsmouth and arrived in perfect weather at its last camp on this side of the Channel.

The day came when the Regiment assembled for their final briefing. Strict security was imposed. The crews were told that within a few days they were to embark for the coast of France.

They were shown maps, which had no place names marked and aerial photographs of beaches and shorelines, as Mr Hennessey recalls: "Our particular targets, which were a line of houses lying back from a beach, were indicated, together with a veritable forest of iron stakes and other impediments embedded in the sands of the beach, visible only at low tide, the majority of which we were told were mined. Suspected enemy gun emplacements were pointed out, together with several other danger spots and we were shown the routes we were to take when once clear of the beach. Finally, we were told the plan for the preliminary air-borne assault, and of the fire support we could expect from the Navy at sea."

The men of the 13th/18th Hussars spent four days at sea on their LCTs while the rest of the armada assembled. Many of the tank crews had no accommodation, although those without bunks were issued with hammocks, very few of which were successfully hung, so the majority bedded down on the hard steel decks next to the tanks.

The LCT is a flat-bottomed craft and so every time it rose up on a wave it would crash back down again, causing the whole ship to shudder and shake. Twice a day they would be visited by the NAAFI launch which was a welcome distraction, although chocolate and sticky buns were hardly what most of them felt they needed in their almost permanent state of seasickness.

By the time June 4th arrived they were all restless at having been imprisoned on their ever-moving ship. There were periods of organised physical training, they cleaned their guns again and again, the crews started and ran the tank engines twice a day creating each time a blue cloud of diesel fumes, which did nothing for their nausea. They each took turns to act as aircraft spotters on the bridge, fortunately never spotting any enemy aircraft, which was just as well, because they would have made a wonderful target for them had they come (Allied air supremacy was one of the prerequisites for the Normandy landings to take place).

At last they learnt that they were to sail that night and the landing was to take place the following morning on 5th June. They were assembled for the final briefing that night and were issued with maps which showed they were headed for the coast of Normandy, to land at the small resort of Lion-sur-mer. The British Division formed part of the left flank of the assault, with the Americans far over to the right. Each man on board the LCT received a copy of an order of the day signed by General Eisenhower and, at 19 years of age, Mr Hennessey remembers how he was caught up in the universal feeling of excitement and pride; "It crossed my mind that 'Gentlemen in England, now in bed, must have felt themselves accursed that they were not here'. I certainly, would not have wished to be anywhere else."

The 4th/7th Royal Dragoon Guards

It was the spring of 1943 when the second regiment to undergo training at Fritton Lake was first told it would be taking part in the assault landing in Operation Overlord, equipped with Amphibious DD Tanks. Early in May they left Keighley, where they had wintered and travelled up to Catterick to learn about the specialist armoured vehicles, which had been developed. This included DD tanks, the AVREs, flails and crocodiles.

The Regiment then moved to Heveningham in Suffolk where it spent the summer and autumn. From here the tank crews were sent a squadron at a time to Great Yarmouth, from where they made the daily journey to Fritton Lake for initial training with DD tanks and the Davis Submerged Escape Apparatus. The tank commanders were converted to 'skippers'. Instead of 'drive right' or 'drive left' they learnt to say 'port 30' or 'starboard 30' and some even learnt to sink the tank. The divisional commander, Major-General Hobart started a lecture one day with the ominous words, "Gentlemen, it is tradition in the Royal Navy that when a ship sinks its captain is automatically court-martialled".

All this training was carried out on and around Fritton Lake, although the Regiment's first encounter with the submerged escape apparatus was in the swimming baths in Nicholas Everritt Park, Oulton Broad. Although top secret at the time, the officer commanding 'B' Squadron, Major Jenkins, recalls in the regimental history how the arrival of the men at the swimming baths was greeted by little boys running round the baths saying "Oh here come the amphibious tanks".

The next session of submerged escape training was to sit in the hull of a Valentine that was placed at the bottom of the concrete well at the Fritton site. Several thousand gallons of water would pour on the Valentine, the crew having just a minute or so to fit the facemask, turn on the oxygen and swim to the surface. The tanks were equipped with a modified version of the apparatus (ATEA) and at Studland Bay they were used in earnest and saved lives during a training accident during exercise 'Smash I' on 4th April 1944.

Valentine DDs aboard a LCT off Gosport.
Imperial War Museum photograph H35172-35187

Valentine DDs at sea off Studland Bay

The names of the following members of the 4th/7th RDG who died during this incident are listed as missing on the memorial at the Brookwood Military Cemetery. Their bodies were never recovered.

Cpl Townson   'B' Squadron
Sgt V Hartley   'C' Squadron   1st Troop
Tpr A Kirby   'C' Squadron   1st Troop
Cpl A Park   'C' Squadron   4th Troop
Tpr E Petty   'C' Squadron   4th Troop

A number of parts have been salvaged from the lost Valentines, including a driver's compass, propeller and war department identity plates. These have been used to help in the restoration of a privately owned Valentine IX DD, War Department No. T8257DD. It is hoped that this Valentine will be fully restored to an operational condition by the summer of 2004.

During the summer a spell at Linney Head firing ranges was completed and one exercise was to fire in line from the water's edge, the first role of the DD tanks on reaching the Normandy beaches. They also did a live exercise with infantry, which was a useful experience as, being in an independent armoured brigade their role was to support the infantry in the close encounter battle. After that the Regiment returned to Suffolk where they were involved in a formation exercise in the Thetford area and in the autumn were able to do some Squadron training with infantry on a small training area nearby. 'B' Squadron carried out this training along with 'C' Company, 1st Battalion The South Lancashire Regiment, commanded by Major Cardozo.

In November 1943 the Regiment left Heveningham and went to Gosport to Fort Monkton, where they took over some Valentine DD Tanks and had their first experience of launching and swimming on the sea. Also for the first time, they practiced loading their tanks onto and launching from LCTs. They operated from Stokes Bay and one night conducted a night launch and swim and a night landing. This was a unique occasion as the whole Regiment was afloat including the RHQ and the commanding officer, Geoffrey Byron. At this point it was decided that only 'B' and 'C' Squadrons would continue with DD tanks. 'A' Squadron and RHQ would be equipped with normal tanks, which would be waterproofed to come ashore from LCTs on the beach.

From Gosport the Regiment went to Scotland, to Fort George, where it spent the Christmas of 1943. From here full-scale landing exercises with Valentine DD Tanks on the Moray Firth were completed, at least one of which included spending the night at sea and launching from LCTs before first light. On the tank park at Fort George Lt Col Jenkins recalls how his gunner let off a blank round one day when the flotation screen was up, resulting in a large round hole in the back of the screen (Valentine DDs had to have their guns facing backwards when the screen was erected due to the length of the gun barrel and its over-hang when facing forwards, which would have made elevating the screen impossible). Fortunately there was a spare screen in stores and the fitters soon had it on the tank.

At Fort George 'A' Squadron and RHQ had their first introduction to waterproofing their tanks for wading, a messy and painstaking job. It was here too that the Regiment first met up with the LCTs, which were to carry them to France on D-Day.

From Fort George the Regiment moved to its old haunts of Chippenham Park near Newmarket, where it stayed briefly before moving south to undertake more training on the Valentine DD at Poole, including landings at Studland Bay. Here they met up again with the LCTs that they had trained with in Scotland.

NEVER FOUND

During the training at Poole the Regiment took part in a series of exercises and landings on Studland Bay, the last of which was a full-scale assault landing watched by General Montgomery and other high ranking officers. During one of the earlier exercises there was a disaster when six tanks were lost and one officer and five other ranks drowned.

Four of the tanks were from 'C' Squadron and two were from 'B' Squadron. It was a landing with two Squadrons up, 'B' on the right and 'C' on the left, which was to be the order of landing on D-Day. The Navy launched the tanks just before first light when the sea was disturbed but considered fit for launching. Almost immediately however, the wind got up and the sea became very rough, the waves buffeting the tanks until in some cases the struts gave way and the screens collapsed.

Lt Ford, the Regiment's intelligence officer, was on one of 'C' Squadrons tanks to get the experience. When the tank went down he managed to escape from the tank by removing the RAF flying boots he was wearing and came up to the surface to be rescued by the Navy. He had a lucky escape but the rest of the crew, including the troop leader, were drowned. One of the 'B' Squadron tanks was blown off course and on to the breakwater between the bay and the Poole channel. It hit the breakwater at an angle and stuck on the top, where it remained for months. Lt Col Jenkins' own tank was also blown off course and got the wrong side of the breakwater that was submerged at that state of the tide. He recalls how they fortunately hit it square on, the driver keeping his foot on the pedal. "As the tracks were revolving the front of the tank rose out of the water getting higher and higher, gradually we motored over the top and down into deep water again the other side and went on to land safely on the beach."

From this disastrous exercise an important lesson was learnt, which was to have great effect on D-Day. Hitherto the decision whether to launch or not to launch DD tanks had been the sole prerogative of the Navy, none of whom had been in a DD tank nor appreciated its lack of buoyancy when the sea was running. Henceforth there was to be an Army officer on board the LCT whose job it would be to advise the Naval commander, although the latter would be the one to make the actual decision. On D-Day on the Regiment's front this officer was Captain David Richards who had done his DD training with 'A' Squadron when they were also equipped with DD tanks.

The sea was rough and accordingly he advised the Naval Commander who sent out the order to the LCTs that they were not to launch the tanks but were to carry out the alternative plan to proceed in to the beach where the tanks would, using their screens, wade ashore. This led to a full complement of tanks reaching the shore with their crews fresh and not exhausted by a long and difficult swim in. Apart from the swim in, another danger to DD tanks swimming ashore on D-Day came from an unexpected quarter. The flotation screen that remained attached to the hull after it had landed could be set alight by tracer bullets and high explosive fire and on D-Day, at least one tank was burnt out from a fire that started this way.

During these exercises on the build up to D-Day the Regiment got to know the sappers who were equipped with AVREs and other devices for dealing with the beach obstacles, including the flail and crocodile tanks. They were scheduled to come into the beach at 'H' hour, just behind the DD tanks and just in front of the infantry.

The final exercise was a full scale landing on Hayling Island, then towards the end of April 'B' and 'C' Squadrons left Poole and moved to Fawley Wood, just inland from Stanswood Bay in the Solent and West of Calshot.

On leaving Poole the Valentine DD tanks were returned to ordnance and the Regiment's operational Sherman DD tanks began to arrive. The Shermans had come straight from America and on unpacking the crews were staggered at the amount of tools and equipment that came with each tank and a large quantity of these tools were deemed to be surplus and were left behind in Fawley Wood.

Sherman DD MK I with auxiliary rear screen or 'apron' photographed
launching at sea. Photograph courtesy of Mr John Pearson

The East Riding Yeomanry (TA Regiment)

Along with the 13th/18th Royal Hussars and the 4th/7th Royal Dragoon Guards, the East Riding Yeomanry formed part of the 27th Armoured Brigade and were the third regiment to be sent for DD training at Fritton Lake. They were initially sent to the Wickham Market area in 1942 and from there to Rendlesham Hall, Suffolk, in April 1943 where they were equipped with conventional Valentine tanks in place of their Covenanters.

Between June and September 1943 the Regiment left their camp a Squadron at a time, to carry out their initial two-week introductory course with the amphibious Valentine DDs at Fritton.

Mr Ray Jones who was a gunner with the East Riding Yeomanry remembers having to sleep under canvas on the Somerleyton estate while undergoing training at Fritton, unlike the 13th/18th Royal Hussars who underwent their initial DD training in April and were accommodated in acquisitioned houses in Great Yarmouth.

By this time a mock-up landing craft ramp had been built out of Bailey bridge components at the edge of the lake, to enable tank crews to practice launching their vehicles as if they were at sea. RAF air reconnaissance photographs show that three of these pontoons had been installed by March 1944.

Unfortunately the regiment experienced a series of mishaps while training at Fritton, demonstrating how dangerous the DD tank could be. The first two accidents are included in the book *Forrard,* the story of the East Riding Yeomanry written by Paul Mace. While driving to the Bailey bridge pontoon with their screens raised at the start of one training session a tank from 'B' Squadron collided with the tank in front of it, tearing its screen. On entering the water this tear opened up and the tank went down in the middle of the lake. Fortunately all of the crew were picked up by the motor launch that was kept nearby in case of such emergencies.

A second incident occurred during one of the particularly hazardous night training exercises. A tank from 'B' Squadron's 3 Troop drove down the ramp too quickly and shipped water, the crew managing to bail out before the tank went down. As a result the troop commander, 2nd Lieutenant G Jenkin who was in a different tank but still responsible for the entire troop, found himself facing a court martial and was prevented from being promoted to full lieutenant for six months.

The only fatal training accident to have happened at Fritton occurred on 22nd June 1943. While driving a Valentine DD, Trooper Leslie Charles Lloyd tragically drowned in the lake. Mr Jones believes Trooper Lloyd's tank may have shipped water as it descended the mock up landing craft ramp. Mr Jones was a close friend of Trooper Lloyds tank commander, Sergeant Charlie Lewsley, who was presented with an award by the Royal Humane Society for attempting to save the life of Trooper Lloyd after the sinking.

Trooper Lloyd had managed to get out of the tank and was on the surface of the water but in a state of extreme panic. Sergeant Lewsley tried to keep him afloat and calm him down, but Lloyd caught hold of Sergeant Lewsley by the neck and the pair went under the surface twice before Sergeant Lewsley managed to break free. Sergeant Lewsley then dived down to try and find Trooper Lloyd, but couldn't find him in the murky waters of the lake. Two months after the incident Sergeant Lewsley travelled to London in his best walking out dress uniform to receive his award from the Royal Humane Society.

Mr Jones recalls that after trooper Lloyd's death it was ordered that the drivers of DD tanks had to be under a specific size, with any 'large' drivers having to stand down from their duties. This was due to the restrictive size of the tank driver's hatch, which made escape difficult.

All of the Valentines lost by the East Riding Yeomanry were recovered shortly and used as a supply of spare parts for the remaining tanks.

Surprisingly, the part of the training that Mr Jones enjoyed most was learning to use the submerged escape apparatus. This began with the crews visiting the large open-air swimming baths at Oulton Broad, just outside Lowestoft. This was done four or five mornings a week, arriving at 06.00 hours under great secrecy and the tightest security possible and departing at 08.00 hours, before the pool opened to the public. The training involved fitting the nose clip, learning to breathe with the apparatus mouthpiece in place and inflating the rubber bag that was strapped to the chest.

Mr Jones, who was a good swimmer, liked to go to the deep end and sit under the ladder to stop him from floating to the surface. Here he would adjust the valve that regulated the amount of oxygen entering the bag until negative buoyancy was achieved. Then he could walk on the bottom, while breathing from the oxygen released into the bag.

Mr Jones recalls the final test at the bottom of the deep concrete well at Fritton Lake, containing the hull of a Valentine tank at its bottom. The tank crew, clad in their denim overalls and wearing gym shoes, would descend into the well by a ladder, wearing the apparatus at the ready but without the mouthpiece in place.

Two concrete pipes from a water tank overhead emptied water into the well, which filled with water at the same rate as it would if the tank was sinking, which is very fast! The cold water made it worse, with the tank crews struggling to catch their breath.

At this point the crew would attach the nose clip, hold the mouthpiece between their teeth and turn the oxygen valve on to fill the rubber bag of the apparatus. They would leave the tank in a specific order, the commander being the first to leave as he was blocking the exit from the turret. The next to go was the driver, then the gunner and lastly the radio operator.

Each man would let enough oxygen into his bag to float to the surface, once there he would inflate the bag sufficiently to keep afloat. At this stage in the development of the DD tank the crews were still being issued with the standard Royal Navy Davis Submerged Escape Apparatus that was also issued to submarine crews.

Other training that Mr Jones took part in at Fritton included the use of the Kelvin Sphere Compass. The compasses, which were provided for both the commander and the driver, were essential if the tanks were to maintain a steady course when at sea in poor visibility or at night.

At the end of January 1944 the Regiment was re-equipped with conventional Sherman tanks and sent to the Moray Firth. The Regiment by this time had been told that it would take part in the Normandy landings using conventional Shermans and not the amphibious DD tanks.

The Nottinghamshire Sherwood Rangers Yeomanry

One of the last British Regiments to be trained for the DD role, not arriving at Fritton Lake until April 1944, the Nottinghamshire Sherwood Rangers Yeomanry were the first Yeomanry ashore on D-Day. Landing two minutes before H hour in their Sherman DDs, the Sherwood Rangers took part in the liberation of Bayeux and was in the thick of the tank fighting around Caen.

The Regiment had arrived back from North Africa in the first half of December 1943, Chippenham Park becoming the Regiment's new home.

Chippenham Park was a delightful country estate surrounded by a park, about five miles from Newmarket. The whole of the 8th Armoured Brigade had been stationed in the park, the beauty of which was spoilt by the erection of Nissen huts and concrete tracks for the tanks. The Regiment was very comfortable and the owner of the estate, a charming old lady, did all she could to add to their comfort.

Soon after their arrival at Chippenham they were informed that the 8th Armoured Brigade, consisting of The Nottinghamshire Sherwood rangers Yeomanry, the 4th/7th Royal Dragoon Guards and the 24th Lancers, would take part in the initial assault of the invasion of north west Europe.

The reception of this news was followed by an extensive period of training and the arrival of reinforcements. The news was received with mixed feelings. They naturally thought they would be used somewhere in north west Europe as they guessed this was why they had been brought back from the Middle East, but the thought of invading Europe in a tank was somewhat alarming.

The Regiment's days at Chippenham Park became extremely hectic once training of the individual reinforcements commenced. This involved teaching the driver to drive the tank, the wireless operator to use and understand his set and to load the 75mm gun, which was one of duties, the gunner to fire and look after his guns, the assistant driver to take over the duties of any other member of the crew at any time and finally the tank commander to direct the driver by means of internal communication when in action, to spot and direct gunfire on to any target and at all times to be in constant wireless communications with his troop leader, and be able to work in tactical co-operation with the other tanks of his troop.

Sound individual basic training was essential for success in any battle and this was followed by Troop, Squadron, Regiment and finally Brigade training, but without sound basic training wireless orders could not be passed effectively between the tanks and the gun could not be fired accurately.

Suddenly news came in that 'B' and 'C' Squadrons were to proceed to an unknown destination and would undergo some special tank training for the invasion. There was considerable secrecy and mystery surrounding this training, which intrigued all in the Regiment and left a certain feeling of apprehension among the members of the two Squadrons concerned.

'A' and 'C' Squadrons had at first been selected for this training, but Michael Laycock the Regimental second in command, told the OIC of 'A' Squadron that as they had already performed the difficult task of leading the Regiment across Africa it had been decided that 'B' Squadron should take their place, a clear indication of the unsavoury nature of what lay ahead.

It wasn't long before 'B' and 'C' Squadrons left for their unknown location, which turned out to be Fritton Lake. During their period of initial DD training at Fritton Lake the personnel were accommodated in the requisitioned boarding houses of Great Yarmouth and Gorleston. As a note of interest, the Regimental historian holds the addresses of several of the crews' billets in these two towns, including the Cliff Hotel, which was also used as the officers' mess of the RAF Air Sea Rescue Service.

Upon arrival at Great Yarmouth 'B' and 'C' Squadrons immediately started their training on Fritton Lake and spent their time waddling their tanks from the shore into the calm water, swimming around and returning to land again.

Stuart Hills, a former tank commander with 'C' Squadron, recalls how the Valentines shipped water alarmingly at Fritton and the bilge pump could barely cope. As if this wasn't enough, there was trouble in the ranks of 'B' Squadron. Although each was highly thought of, the Squadron leader and his driver just didn't get on. Feeling particularly aggrieved at the leader's comments one day at practice, when the order to turn to port was made the driver collapsed the screen instead, the DD tank plunging to the bottom of the lake. There were no casualties and the tank was later recovered.

Mr Hills recalls that the part of their training they feared the most was using the submerged escape apparatus. "Our ears thumped under the pressure and it was pitch dark, so that I had to tap each man on the shoulder to tell him it was his turn to swim to the surface. Some men found the whole business very disconcerting, especially the non-swimmers and several flatly refused to enter the tank in spite of direct orders and threats".

"Each man had to don the apparatus and then descend into a specially constructed well filled with water, into which the hull of a tank had been sunk. Six men flatly refused to do this, in spite of orders, pep talks and threats. In the end Michael Laycock, the Regimental second in command, was summoned to deal with the situation.

He addressed them in his usual energetic and sincere way, pointed out the simplicity of the operation and proceeded to demonstrate. All went well until he had surfaced, then in his eagerness and enthusiasm he removed the escape apparatus in the wrong sequence, which was the only part of the whole operation which required care and, if not done correctly caused a certain amount of coughing and spluttering.

The effect of the demonstration was somewhat marred by a fit of choking, spluttering and gasping. Despite this, through his perseverance, good humour and tact, he managed to dispel all the doubts and fears of those who had refused and nearly all went down."

Those who were found to be 'unsuitable' for working with DD tanks were transferred to a new unit and replaced with a fresh draft. Mr Hills' own tank driver only joined his crew because the original driver had been one of the men who refused to carry out the underwater escape training and was subsequently transferred out of the Squadron.

Mr Arthur Reddish recalls one amusing incident that occurred during training with the submerged escape apparatus. "The model used was a modified version of the one used by submarine crews. For the final test, each crew in turn manned a tank sat at the bottom of a huge chamber. Then valves opened and water poured in, barely giving us time to adjust the apparatus before the water was over our heads."

"Eventually, the pressure was great and we had to hang on to our seats to prevent being forced to the surface. After many long minutes, a light came on indicating the ordeal was over and we could return to the surface. Breathing through a tube in the mouth with the nose and ears plugged proved to be scary stuff."

Mr Reddish remembers one amusing event that occurred during the under-water escape training: "During training one day a 'stranger' was observed underwater taking a profound interest in all our doings. The entire operation was secret and the intruder was approached as he left the water. To our great glee, it turned out to be Captain Hylda Young, our medical officer. Hylda was one of the Regiment's characters. "I only wanted to see what you chaps are up to," he explained. Presumably, our doctor had noted the inordinate number appearing on his sick parades complaining of neuralgia!"

The Regimental history records how the men underwent this "completely unexpected and somewhat dangerous training with their usual philosophical good humour," but there were a few who complained that whereas they were quite willing to continue to fight in a tank on land they were not prepared "to be a bloody sailor in a bloody tank".

An effort was made to obtain danger pay for those who were to fight in a DD tank on D-Day, a reasonable request in view of the numerous Naval personnel who are granted danger pay during wartime. Although this request had the support of many of the Regiment's officers it was not looked upon favourably by the War Office.

After Great Yarmouth, the Regiment was sent to the South Coast, to Lee-On-Solent, for training on Sherman DDs. Working in close co-operation with the Navy they tried launching their tanks from LCTs and soon learnt to appreciate the difficulties of stray currents, gusty winds and falling tides.

Once clear of the landing craft ramp, the driver would engage third gear and head for the beach. The driver could tell when the tank was sea-borne because of a white tube on his dashboard, similar to a condom, which was kept inflated by the pressure of the water. This device was more useful when the tank was leaving the water, as it informed the driver when he could safely drop the screen without swamping the tank. Although the freeboard of the Sherman DD was higher than that of the Valentine, it did not prevent the tank from shipping a good deal of water when the sea was choppy.

As part of its operational amphibious training the Regiment 'invaded' several beaches on the south coast, often under the cover of a smoke screen, and later a beach on the Isle of Wight below Osborne Castle, a former residence of Queen Victoria.

Meanwhile 'A' Squadron, the Regiment's non-amphibious Squadron, had been equipped with new Sherman tanks, some armed with the new 17-pounder gun. Training took place over all types of country and in all weathers, which was to prove invaluable later.

Finally the Regiment was parked in a forest in Fawley, right on the sea opposite the Isle of Wight. This was towards the end of May. Here the amphibious squadrons were issued with their invasion equipment, brand new Sherman DDs for the D-Day landing. They had to be fitted with alternative radio sets, as those that came with the tank were not familiar to the British crews. Here at the camp they found themselves virtually imprisoned and forbidden to leave. The food at the camp was reportedly 'marvellous' and all of them knew what lay ahead and that many would not survive.

The Squadrons were issued with maps of the invasion beaches but for the moment the real names of the places were withheld for security reasons. The Germans expected the invasion in the Calais area over the shortest channel crossing. On the evening of June 3rd they embarked in their tank Troops, three tanks to a Troop and they stood at Southampton Water opposite the Isle of Wight.

The Staffordshire Yeomanry

Although not trained for or equipped with DD tanks for the Normandy landings, the Staffordshire Yeomanry were equipped with Sherman DDs for river crossing operations later in the war, so it is reasonable to mention their preparations for D-Day. In 1944, after returning from the battle of El Alamein in the autumn of 1943, the Brigade re-assembled at Chippenham Park, Newmarket under the command of Brigadier J. M. Anstice D.S.O. and were told of the part they were to play in the forthcoming invasion of Europe. In order to even out the Regiments with recent battle experience among the Brigades, which had not fought since France in 1940, certain changes were now made. The Staffordshire Yeomanry changed places with the 4th/7th Royal Dragoon Guards in the 27th Armoured Brigade and the 3rd Battalion Royal Tank Regiment replaced the 24th Lancers in the 29th Armoured Brigade now commanded by Brigadier Harvey. Brigadier Bernard Cracroft now assumed command of the 8th Armoured Brigade, which was composed as follows.

4th/7th Royal Dragoon Guards, 24th Lancers, Nottinghamshire Yeomanry (Sherwood Rangers), 147th Field Regiment (Essex Yeomanry) Royal Artillery, 12th Battalion The King's Royal Rifle Corps, 168th (City of London) Light Field Ambulance, 552nd Company Royal Army Service Corps, 8th Armoured Brigade Workshops REME and 265th Forward Delivery Squadron.

Intensive training in combined operations followed while all staffs were deeply immersed in the planning of operation 'Overlord', the assault on Normandy.

The 4th/7th Royal Dragoon Guards had already completed a stiff course of training in the secret DD swimming tank with the 27th Armoured Brigade and two Squadrons of the Sherwood Rangers Yeomanry went to Fritton in Norfolk to carry out a similar course during March 1944.

April saw feverish activity when all equipment had to be waterproofed, the non-DD tanks, including the Shermans of the Staffordshire Yeomanry, being equipped to wade in six feet of water. All training culminated in exercise 'Fabius' in early May when a full-scale rehearsal of the landing was carried out.

On 19th May the Brigade moved to its concentration area at Hursley Park, near Winchester and on 1st June all units were 'sealed' into transit camps in the Romsey area. The air of England was heavy with pent-up excitement and expectancy.

Canadian DD Units of The 3rd Canadian Infantry Division

To carry out the assault on Juno beach, the area between the British target beaches of *Gold* and *Sword,* was the 3rd Canadian Infantry Brigade, under the command of Major-General Roderick Keller, who was seriously injured by an American bombing on 8th August 1944.

In support of the infantry were various independent units representing the various 'funnies' of the 79th Armoured Division, including DD tanks manned by the 6th and 10th Canadian Armoured Regiments (the Fort Garry Horse and the 1st Hussars).

The 10th Canadian Armoured Regiment (The Fort Gary Horse) was mobilised on 3rd September 1939, after Britain's declaration of war on Germany, with Canada officially declaring war on the 10th September. The Regiment was initially given the task of Divisional Cavalry Regiment for the 2nd Canadian Division. Troop Sergeant Frank (Paddy) Hutton was a tank commander with 'B' Squadron of the Fort Garry Horse from September 1939 to November 1944, and in a story originally told in the CFB Calgary Newspaper of 3rd May 1995, he tells of his involvement with DD tanks.

Originally they were issued with Valentine tanks, carrying out their initial DD training on Valentines that had been converted to the Duplex Drive configuration in the Great Yarmouth and Gosport areas under great secrecy and typically at night. Once launched on the water, the line of DD tanks followed a light on a leading 'P' boat, each tank also having a light on its stern for the next amphibious tank to follow.

In the spring of 1944 the Fort Garry Horse were issued with Sherman DD tanks to replace their Valentines (they originally had normal Sherman tanks before training on Valentines). On 2nd June 1944 the Regiment boarded their landing craft with their over loaded Sherman DDs (extra ammo) and tied up to buoys in the Southampton Seaway. Mr Hutton recalls how the seas on D-Day were dreadful and the actual landings were postponed for some time. Finally, after three days on the ship, the crossing was made and the crews awoke to prepare their swimming tanks by inflating the air support tubes and attaching the support struts. By the time the screens were erected they could see the shore and hear the shooting.

The 6th Canadian Armoured Regiment (1st Hussars) disembarked from HMS Oronsay at Liverpool on 22nd November, arriving at Aldershot the same day. After being issued with the new Sherman tank the Regiment moved to Scotland for a period of live firing exercises on 23rd September 1943. Selection as a DD Regiment saw the Regiment receive 20 Valentine tanks for training on the 22nd November 1943 and, once familiar with these, 'A' and 'B' Squadrons were moved to Great Yarmouth between 6th and 21st December 1943, for secretive training with the Valentine DD. While at Great Yarmouth, the Regiment threw a Christmas party for 376 local children.

On 1st January 1944 it was confirmed that the Regiment would take part in the D-Day landings. With this task in mind, 'A' and 'B' Squadrons moved south to Fort Monkton, Gosport, for intensive operational training with the DD tank.

After a productive period of training with 7th Canadian Infantry Brigade, and more field firing at Warcrop ranges, 'A' and 'B' Squadrons were sent to a secret location known as 'Shangri-La' for more DD training, returning early for inspection on 19th February 1944. By April, all of the Regiment's RAM Mk II tanks had been replaced with Shermans and waterproofing of these had begun in earnest. The last practice amphibious operation started on 29th April 1944 and lasted until 6th May.

US DD Units

As well the British and Canadian Regiments that were equipped with DD tanks, three American Tank Battalions (70th, 741st and 743rd) were also trained in their use for the Normandy invasion. The unit book of the 743rd notes that in December 1944, 'B' and 'C' Companies were sent to an unknown location for training in the use of the British Valentine tanks and that in January those same Companies were sent to Great Yarmouth to participate in special training with the DD version of the Valentine. This training lasted throughout May and included training at Gosport and a series of 'dry runs' at Torcross between April and May 1944, the Battalions now being equipped with Sherman DD tanks. On 2nd June 1944 the tanks were loaded onto LCTs for the invasion.

The US Army Sherman DD that now stands over-looking the beach at Slapton, Dorset.
Sadly little remains of the external DD equipment on this tank

The 'History of The 70th Tank Battalion' mentions the training on DD tanks, noting that on 4th March 1944 'A' and 'B' Companies "slipped away for a session of top-secret training with what later developed to be the DD tank". On 1st April 1944 'A' Company departed for special training with the DD tanks, followed by 'B' and 'C' Company on 6th and 13th April respectively. The book also mentioned the installation of the canvas floats and propellers (presumably on the Sherman DD tanks) at Lupton Camp, near Torquay in late April 1944.

Although the exact location of the training is not recorded in this book, a second book (Strike Swiftly, Marvin Jenson, 1997) sheds more light on their training. 'A' and 'B' Companies were sent to Great Yarmouth for training with the DD tank. Initial training was with the Valentine DD tank, as the Sherman DDs had not yet arrived. The book mentions a 'pond on the edge of the North Sea' (Fritton Lake), where the training with Valentines was conducted. Training finished on about 14th March 1944. In early April the two Companies of the 70th went to the staging area, where they received 32 Sherman DD tanks.

These were not the only American Tank Battalions to be equipped with the Sherman DD. The American DD tanks that survived D-Day were shipped to Italy where three other battalions, the 191st, 753rd and 756th were preparing for the invasion of Southern France, the 753rd and 756th training at Salerno, while the 191st trained in the Bay of Naples. Another battalion, the 736th, supported American forces during the crossing of the Rhine in 1945.

Recently an US Army Sherman DD was discovered in the Gulf of Salerno, about a mile offshore when an underwater cameraman came across its remains. Regina Sansalone, an Ohio nursery school teacher who was working for a documentary film company in Italy, sent footage to US military authorities.

In 2002 the rescue and salvage ship Grasp recovered the sunken Sherman about a mile offshore. Eventually, it was identified as a Sherman DD from the 753rd Tank Battalion of the 7th Army that had lost one of its tanks during training when a projection from the landing craft ripped its screen, drowning one crewman. It is hoped that the tank will be transported back to America and put on permanent display there at the Patton Museum of Armour.

Another American casualty was the Sherman DD pictured on the previous page. This tank was lost while taking part in Operation Tiger, the D-Day practice landings at Slapton Sands in 1944 and was only recovered in 1984. It now stands next to a public car park in Slapton as a permanent memorial to the American lives lost during the course of these practice landings.

The tank was lost during the tragic climax to an invasion exercise that had itself gone disastrously wrong. South of Dartmouth, near the village of Slapton Sands on the South Devon Coast, one of ten simulated landings had taken place that morning. The target, a coarse gravel beach stretching out towards a sheltered lagoon, was a credible substitute for Normandy. The landings, Operations Duck, Parrot, Beaver, Tiger and the six part Operation Fabius, were designed as a dress rehearsal for the beaches called Omaha and Utah.

But at 5am on 28th April 1944 General Eisenhower, along with Tedder, Montgomery, Bradley and Ramsay (each man aboard separate craft for reasons of security) had watched Operation Tiger fall apart. For reasons unknown, the Hawker Typhoon fighters, due to swoop over the invaders at H-hour, never arrived over the target. The skippers of many LCTs, ignoring all signals from the engineers already ashore, landed where they chose. The troops disembarking from the LCIs ambled ashore, discarding their bedrolls at any convenient spot on the beach.

It was not until late on the night of April 28th, however, that Eisenhower realised just how badly Operation Tiger had gone, for 749 men were already dead. It had probably happened as early as 1.30am when convoy T-4, a straggling 80-strong assembly of LSTs spread out over three miles, was moving at a leisurely six knots through the darkness of Lyme Bay. Thirty-three miles ahead lay their destination, Slapton Sands. At the same time, nine E-boats of Kapitan zur Zee Rudolph Peterson's Cherbourg based 5th and 9th Schnelleboote Flotillas, on a routine night patrol, sighted their prey. Closing in at 35 Knots, on powerful Daimler-Benz engines, their torpedoes sought and found three of the wallowing LSTs. Red and green tracer seared the night and many young soldiers, hearing the order abandon ship jumped to their deaths, ignorant even of how to inflate their Mae West lifebelts.

Among the missing US servicemen were ten officers classed as bigots, the codename for the small number of officers who knew the details of the planned Normandy landings. Fortunately none of these men fell into German hands and all ten bodies were recovered within a week of the disaster.

Chapter Five

D-Day

A Sherman DD of the 13th/18th Royal Hussars abandoned in the surf. No doubt this tank gave much needed fire support to the infantry on *Sword Beach* before being swamped by the advancing tide. The Commander's steadying post and the bracket for the Kelvin Sphere magnetic compass can be seen at the rear of the turret

On the morning of 6th June 1944, the crews who had spent the previous years and months training on the DD tanks finally had the opportunity to put that training into practice. For the first time in history tanks were to lead an assault from the sea, on all sectors of the beaches. Sadly the weather was to prevent many of the tank crews from taking the opportunity to put their special training and equipment to the test.

At *Gold Beach*, the order was given to carry out the secondary plan to land the DD tanks as close to the shore as possible. But in spite of being launched just a hundred yards or so from the beach, the 4th/7th Royal Dragoon Guards lost five and the Sherwood Rangers Yeomanry lost eight in the breakers. At *Utah Beach* the tanks of the American 70th Tank Battalion were all launched 3,000 yards from the shore, resulting in the loss of just one tank. At *Sword Beach* the tanks of the 13th/18th were perhaps the most successful of the DD units on D-Day, in that they launched from 5,000 yards from the coast with 31 of the 34 tanks launched safely reaching the shore.

The secret of the Duplex Drive had been well kept and the early and unexpected arrival of armour had a remarkable effect on the enemy, with the result that opposition was lighter than had been expected.

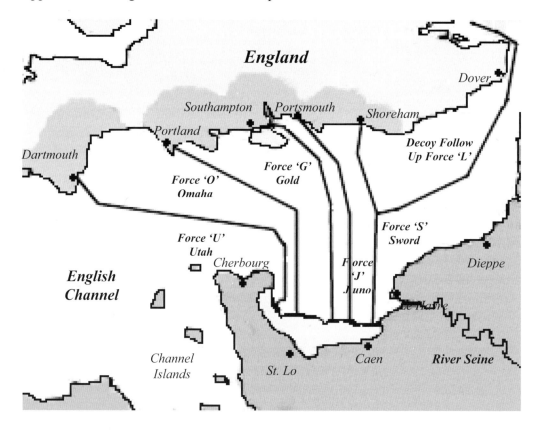

Sector	Assault Formation	DD Units	Action
Utah	4th U.S Infantry Division with one Regimental Combat Team up	70th Tank Battalion	30 tanks launched at 3,000 yards. One foundered.
Omaha	1st U.S Infantry Division with two Regimental Combat Teams up	743rd Tank Battalion	Not launched. All beached direct from LCTs.
		741st Tank Battalion	29 tanks launched at 6,000 yards. 2 swam in. 3 beached from LCTs.
Gold	50th British Infantry Division with two Brigade Groups up (231 Brigade with 47 Commando and 69 Brigade)	Notts. Sherwood Rangers Yeomanry, 4th/7th RDG (8th Armoured Brigade)	Not launched. All beached from LCTs on orders.
Juno	3rd Canadian Infantry Division with two Brigade Groups up	6th Canadian Armoured Regiment (1st Hussars)	'A' Squadron launched 10 at 1,500 – 2,000 yards.
		(7th Canadian Brigade & 8th Canadian Brigade)	7 tanks touched down on beach. Another 6 tanks beached from LCTs.
			'B' Squadron launched 19 tanks at 4,000 yards of which 14 reached the shore.
		10th Canadian Armoured Regiment (Fort Garry Horse)	Not launched. All beached from LCTs.
Sword	3rd British Infantry Division with one Brigade Group up (8 Infantry Brigade) and Commando Brigades on each flank	13th/18th Royal Hussars (27th Armoured Brigade)	40 tanks embarked. 6 failed to launch. 34 launched at 5,000 yards. 3 sank during swim in, 31 reached shore.

Combined Operations Pilotage Parties

A special mention needs to be made of the task performed by the Combined Operations Pilotage Parties (COPPs) who had the unenviable task of leading the first wave of DD tanks onto the beaches. Lt Cdr Nigel Clogstoun-Willmott, a Royal Navy navigation specialist was put in charge of raising teams specifically for beach reconnaissance and assault force navigation. The first unit was formed in 1942 and the personnel of each unit included a Royal Navy / Royal Navy Reserve Lt Cdr or Lt (navigation or hydrography specialist), a maintenance officer, an electrical mechanic, Royal Navy paddlers, a Royal Engineers draftsman, a Royal Engineers officer and a commando corporal to act as guard to the RE officer.

Besides the varied personnel each unit was issued with specialist equipment, most of which was unheard of at the time including waterproof watches, under-water writing tablets, underwater torches, infra-red homing gear, special swimsuits and waterproof kit of all kinds.

When piloting an assault landing the COPPs would flash their torches and infra-red beacons from submarines and canoes, while other members were in the leading landing craft. From the summer of 1943 their biggest commitment was the preparation for the Normandy invasion. Clogstoun-Willmott was in personal command, leading COPP 1. Teams were launched both from x-craft (midget submarines) and from LCNs (Assault Landing Craft converted for navigation).

On 6th June 1944 COPPs 1 and 9 were offshore marking from x-craft, while COPP 6 used two assault boats to pilot in the leading armoured troops in the DD tanks, right onto the beaches.

In 1945 COPPs 5 and 7 were employed to aid in the crossing of the Rhine and Elbe in Germany.

Utah Beach

An intense naval and air bombardment was to take place before the main beach assault began, the DD tanks leading the way in. The various sapper formations were scheduled to land close behind the infantry to clear beach obstructions and to blow gaps in the low sea wall paralleling the beach. The landing of the 32 DD tanks at *Utah* was delayed when one of the control ships struck a mine and sunk and, nearby, four DD tanks were lost when the LCT carrying them sank before they could be launched. In contrast to the heavy losses off *Omaha*, twenty-eight DD tanks made it to the beach and provided invaluable supporting fire for the infantry already ashore.

Omaha Beach

At *Easy Red Sector* of *Omaha Beach* Companies E and F of the 2nd Battalion, 16th Infantry Division were to land in the first wave. They were to have been preceded by Company B of the 741st Tank Battalion (Sherman DDs), followed by the 18th Regimental Combat Team at H hour plus 195 minutes. Of the four tanks that made it ashore, one was hit immediately. The remainder of Company B's tanks foundered in the channel. Only one boat section from each infantry company waded ashore on *Easy Red*, losing much of their equipment in the neck-deep water.

On *Omaha Beach Easy Red Sector.* A Sherman DD tank with its rear screen section still in the raised position can be seen in the centre left of the picture, with deep-water wading tanks to either side

At *Omaha Beach Dog Green Sector*, made famous in the film 'Saving Private Ryan', the initial assault was carried out by three units: Company B, 743rd Tank Battalion (sixteen DD tanks). Company A, 116th Infantry (six boat sections in LCAs followed by a command boat) and three LCMs (Landing Craft Mechanized) carrying units of the 146th Special Engineer Task Force, all coming ashore at about 06.30 hours. The collective stories of these units make one aware of how near defeat the landing at *Omaha Beach* was during its first hours.

The tanks of Company B suffered first, the heavy seas preventing the DDs launching offshore. During the effort to bring them directly to the beach one of the LCTs was sunk by German fire and half of the Company's tanks and all but one of its officers were lost. The eight surviving Sherman DDs began their fire mission at the water's edge. The infantry's boat sections also suffered crippling losses before they hit the beach. LCA 5 foundered a thousand yards offshore and five soldiers drowned in the rough sea. No one saw LCA 6 go down, but there were no survivors and only half the bodies were recovered.

Gold Beach

In the plan for the assault on D-Day the 89th Armoured Brigade was to support the 50th Northumbrian Division, with the 4th/7th Royal Dragoon Guards in support of the 69th Infantry Brigade. For the landing on *Gold Beach*, 'B' Squadron of the 4th/7th Royal Dragoon Guards were on the right in support of the 6th Green Howards, while 'C' Squadron were on the left in support of the 5th East Yorks. 'A' Squadron were to land later and support the 7th Green Howards in their further advance.

Then, out to sea were the Brigade's SP artillery Regiment, who would be firing from their LCTs from way back behind the launching position and this of course would all be preceded by the naval and air bombardment.

The maps for the D-Day landings were in sealed bundles on board the LCTs and were not opened until at sea, a very queasy job in the heaving cabin of an LCT. As the flotilla of ships rounded the Needles the decision was taken to postpone the invasion by 24 hours. Postponement caused a major security problem as there were only three days when the tides would be right for the landings to take place, as they would not have been right again for about two weeks. As it turned out the gales were much worse two weeks later.

On D-Day the launching position for the DD tanks was to be 5,000 yards from the beach. In the run up the LCTs would proceed with each Division in line ahead on parallel courses, each Division keeping station with the next. Just before reaching the launching position each Division would come into a line abreast formation, then they would stop. The ramp would be lowered and the tanks would move off into the water.

The group of tanks in each of the Squadron's three LCTs was under the command of one of the Squadron HQ officers, either the Squadron Leader, the Second-in-Command or the Reconnaissance Officer respectively. Squadron HQ was therefore split between the three groups, with the tanks of each of these officers positioned at the rear in the LCT up against the bridge. The LCT captain was then able to communicate with the HQ officer via a long wireless cable that ran down to his tank. His tank was therefore the first on and the last off. The Squadron leader would be with the senior LCT commander. In the case of Lt Col Jenkins (Squadron Leader of 'B' Squadron) he was with Lt Cdr Evans, who was also the LCT flotilla commander.

The task of the DD tanks on landing was to stand at the water's edge, where they would get some cover from the water that came up to the level of the tracks and to drench the German defences sited immediately behind the beach with HE and machine-gun fire. This would give covering fire and support to the breaching teams while they were dealing with the beach obstacles and the minefields on the beach and then to the first wave of infantry in their assault across the beach.

As soon as there was a lane through the minefield and two lanes were made on each Squadron front, the DD tanks would move off the beach, marry up with the infantry and continue to support them in their attacks on the defences and gun emplacements in the area behind the beach. Communications with the infantry was by the number 18 radio set in the Squadron Leader's tank. These sets had been 'netted' (networked) by the signals before D-Day, but unfortunately they had been switched over and Lt Col Jenkins found himself talking to the 5th East Yorks on 'C' Squadron's front while 'C' Squadron was talking to the 6th Green Howards.

On D-Day the DD tank deployment that had been practiced for so long did not happen due to the bad weather, which forced the alternative plan to be adopted. Under this plan the LCTs with the DD tanks on board would wait at the launching position and allow the LCTs with the breaching teams and the LCAs with the first wave of infantry to pass through them. They would then fall in behind and proceed to the beach where, on touchdown the tanks would wade ashore with their screens raised, allowing them to be landed in much deeper water than an ordinary tank waterproofed for wading. This helped the LCTs to make a quick getaway so as not to impede the waves of craft coming in behind them.

Relieved of the effort of a long swim into the beach, the tank crews had a wonderful spectators' view of the landing, which was made all the more spectacular by the bright clear morning as Lt Col Jenkins recalls: "We could see the landing craft ahead and we could see the waves of aircraft going in to attack the enemy positions and we could hear the fire from the destroyers and from the SP Sextons firing from their LCTs back behind them."

"There is no doubt that the decision not to launch that day was the right one. The sea would have caused many casualties and prevented a full complement of tanks reaching the shore. On the beach 'B' Squadron suffered two tank casualties. One tank was swamped in a shell hole, the other went up on a mine, but their crews were unhurt. The AVREs and flails soon had the lanes open through the minefields and they were able to move off the beach.

We went past the bus shelter, which on the air photographs had looked like a pillbox and up the track past the white house with the circular drive. We concentrated on the high ground above through Ver-sur-mer and married up with the infantry to support them in the advance inland."

With the landing on *Gold Beach* came the end of the Regiment's involvement with the DD tank. All surviving Sherman DDs from the landing were quickly sent back to ordnance, the Regiment receiving normal Shermans in their place.

The Sherwood Rangers Yeomanry were also to land on *Gold Beach*. Philip Foster, who was a crewman on a Sherman DD that took part in the assault on *Gold Beach* gives the following account of the action in his book, 'A Trooper's Desert War': "So that night the armada set sail for Normandy, a whole night's crossing. We were all issued with anti-sea sickness pills. We also carried packs of iron rations containing things like cubes of tea, milk and sugar combined, as well as self-heating tins of soup and cocoa."

"All night we proceeded across the channel, aiming for *Gold Beach* in the Bayeux sector on the extreme right of the British invasion. Immediately to their right were the Americans aiming for *Omaha Beach*."

"By morning our tank commander, acting sergeant Bill Digby, was rather green in the face and felt somewhat queasy. Daylight had arrived and we could see the coast approaching from our LCT with its cargo of the three tanks of our troop. The original plan to launch the tanks at sea, about five miles out from the coast, had to be abandoned due to the weather conditions. In the end we slid off the ramps into the sea only about half a mile from the shore, with the beach clearly visible ahead. It was about 7.30am, and I noticed a Navy rocket ship further in, blasting off endless clusters of rockets into the hinterland."

"This gave us some feeling of encouragement that the Germans' defences were being hammered. We had been briefed the previous day that their defences were to have been destroyed by allied aircraft before the landings, but it soon became evident that the Germans, from their surviving static defences were now greeting the tanks and landing craft with a pounding as they swam forward. We had a nasty moment when one of the steel struts supporting the screen became detached, causing the screen to billow inwards. Fortunately the tank commander managed to climb out of his turret onto the deck of the tank, and managed to force the strut back into place. The tank proceeded safely through the rain of shells right onto the beach, as we had so often done in practice."

"Now on firm ground and facing up the beach, I could see through my periscope over the dunes the little village of Le Hamel intact and seemingly deserted, any inhabitants lying low in fear of their lives. The Germans of course, had the beach covered with their guns and there was probably a strongpoint ahead of us, enfilading the beach. Over the wireless tuned into the Regiment's frequency we heard the Troop Commander, Lt Horley say in an anxious voice that his tank was on fire. Then we heard no more as the Troop Commander's tank was knocked out and he was killed."

"We continued on and fired our first shell, but then things went wrong for us. Ahead the Germans had an anti-tank gun that started firing at quite close range. The next moment the tank was hit by an armour piercing shell, probably 50mm, which penetrated the three inch thick turret just in front of the gunner. The shell passed through the knee of the gunner, taking both of the commander's legs off above the knees, and hitting me in the foot. Mercifully the tank didn't catch fire, as Shermans are prone to do and the driver started to back up. The driver's limited visibility meant he couldn't see properly where he was going and we ended up stuck in the surf at the water's edge, unable to move forwards or backwards."

"The only thing we could do was to try and get out of the tank, not an easy task with three wounded men in the turret. I found I could walk without feeling any pain as my foot had gone numb and we managed to climb out of the tank and carry the commander up the beach, taking refuge behind a knocked out tank."

Mr Foster had already given a morphine injection to the tank commander while they were in the tank and they lay there in sand for ten hours, waiting for medical help to arrive. About 5pm prisoners started coming past and stretcher bearers arrived to take the wounded back along the beach and over a field to a dressing station. Here they stayed for two days before a flat-bottomed ship came in to take the casualties back to England.

Mr Foster's tank commander died the day after he received his injuries.

REME Sherman Beach Armoured Recovery Vehicle (BARV). This deep wading vehicle would have been used to tow 'drowned' tanks ashore during the invasion to reduce the risk to incoming landing craft. It could also be used to push stranded Landing Craft back out to sea. When in operational use the BARV would have two railway sleeper sized planks of wood attached to its front to act as a fender when pushing other vehicles out of the water. Approximately 60 Sherman BARVs were ordered and most were completed before D-Day. Each of the eight British Beach Recovery Sections (REME element of the Beach Groups) was established to hold six BARVs but not all were fully equipped by D-Day. Two of the beach groups were sent to each of the three 'British' beaches under the command of HQ Beach Sub Area, the remaining two beach groups being held in reserve. Photograph reproduced courtesy of the REME Museum of Technology

Juno Beach

The Sherman DDs making it ashore at *Juno Beach* provided vital fire support for 'A' Company of the Regina Rifles, which encountered heavy fire both from the German resistance nests in the harbour and from artillery positioned further inland. Near the port area of Courseulles-sur-mer stands a Sherman DD, recovered in 1971. Belonging to the 6th Canadian 1st Armoured Regiment (1st Hussars), this tank is one of five (out of nineteen) that foundered on the run in. Tank *Bold*, of 'B' Squadron, was recovered offshore a few years ago and is now a permanent near the beach at Courselles, being the only surviving Canadian Sherman DD.

On 26th May 1944, the officers of the 1st Hussars were briefed on the invasion, and began the co-ordination of plans with the 3rd Canadian Infantry Division. The Sherman DDs of 'A' and 'B' Squadrons were loaded on LCTs at Bayhouse, while RHQ and 'C' Squadron (deep wading Shermans) boarded ships at Gosport, arriving at Southampton the same day.

On 5th June 1944 the ships left for the French coast, 'A' and 'B' Squadrons landing at Courselles-sur-mer on 6th June at 07.30 hours in support of the 7th Canadian Infantry Brigade. While assisting the infantry to clear the German resistance, the Sherman DDs accounted for 16 guns destroyed, including eight 88mm guns, several light-armoured and non-armoured vehicles shot up and heavy casualties inflicted on the German infantry. During this action the Regiment suffered only light casualties in the form of twenty-two men killed. One troop of 'C' Squadron reached the Caen-Bayeux railway and became the only Allied unit to succeed in reaching its objectives on D-Day, pulling back and regrouping at Pierrepont that evening.

The 10th Canadian Armoured Regiment (Fort Garry Horse) also landed on *Juno Beach,* 'B' and 'C' Squadrons landing at Bernieres-sur-mer and at St. Aubin-sur-mer respectively. Because of the bad weather the Royal Navy operating the LCTs insisted on launching the tanks as close to the shore as possible. Because of this all of 'B' Squadron's 18 Sherman DDs reached the shore in safety.

Once ashore, the crews dropped the screen and cut it away in order to bring the tank's bow machine-gun to bear and, once past the breached seawall, the tanks continued inland with the supporting infantry.

British or Canadian Infantry advancing with the support of Sherman DD tanks

Sword Beach

Once again the DD tanks proved their worth. Members of No. 4 Commando and two Free French Troops of No. 10 Commando, fighting their way inland from *Sword Beach* through Riva-Bella, were stopped by concentrated fire from the casino and its adjoining house. Only after a DD tank had been called up from the beach were the commandos able to silence the defenders.

The assault on the beaches which were dominated by the forts of Ouistram and under fire of the guns of both le Havre and the batteries at Houlgate, away to the east of the mouth of the river Orne, was carried out by the 13th/18th Hussars in DD tanks. Two Squadrons of this Regiment supporting on the right the 9th and on the left the 8th Infantry Brigade, launched from LCTs two and a half miles out to sea. Thirty-four of the tanks entered the water, one, failing to engage its propellers, was immediately overcome by the waves and sunk. Two more were run down by LCTs while swimming for the shore.

Thirty-one tanks reached the beach. They were quickly joined by wading AVREs and Flail Tanks and it is reported that all aimed fire on *Sword Beach*, other than that of small arms fire, had been silenced by H hour plus 20 minutes.

A number of DD tanks were overcome by the crashing waves and the rapidly rising tide that swamped their engines. These tanks remained in action however, and the crews only baled out when the guns themselves became awash. Their crews covered the remaining 200 to 300 yards to the beach in the rubber aircraft dinghies carried by the DD tanks, which saved many lives that day.

The following is an account by Group Captain Patrick Hennessey MBE, RAF (Retd), who served as a Lance-Corporal Gunner Operator with The 13th/18th Royal Hussars (Queen Mary's Own) during the assault on *Sword Beach.*

"As daylight slowly appeared on the morning of 5th June 1944 we could see ships of every description stretching away to the horizon on both sides of us and to the rear. It was a stupendous sight that must remain in the memory of all who saw it. We marvelled that such a gigantic force could assemble over a period of five days and move across the English Channel undetected."

"We were at last given the order to board the tanks. We climbed on, stowed away bedding rolls and made sure that everything was in its place, then took post to inflate the screen. The air bottle was turned on and the screen began to rise. We took particular care to make sure the struts were secure because the effect of the large waves could be felt against the LCT and we were under no illusions what they would do to a puny DD tank once it got into the water."

"The bombardment began with a tremendous roar of gunfire. On our left we heard a terrifying 'whooshing' sound as a rocket firing ship (LCR) went into action, the burning projectiles carving an arc through the sky as they sped towards the shore. Beyond her stood HMS Warspite adding a loud contribution from her large guns."

"We heard the order over the ship's tannoy, "Down door, No.1" and we knew this was our cue. The ramp on the bow of our LCT was lowered into the sea, the ship hove to, tank engines started and Sergeant Rattle's tank moved forward and nosed into the waves. We followed and, as we righted in the water I could just see the shoreline some 5,000 yards away! It seemed a very long distance and in a DD tank, in that sea, it was!"

"The crew were all on deck apart from Harry Bone who was crouched in the driving compartment, intent on keeping the engine running because, as we all knew, if that stopped we stood no chance of survival. The noise seemed to increase and the sea appeared even rougher from this low point of view, with a certain amount of water being shipped. The assistant driver, whose job it was to man the bilge pump, was kept hard at work throughout the crossing."

"Each side of us other DD tanks were launching. To my right and behind me I watched a tank as it came down the ramp and into the sea. It straightened up and began to make way, but behind it I could see the large bulk of its LCT creeping forward. The distance between them closed and in a very few minutes the inevitable happened, the bows of the LCT struck the DD tank and forced it under the water. The tank disappeared and was never seen again. The commander, standing on his platform behind the turret, managed to escape and was picked up, but the rest of the crew were lost."

"It was a struggle to keep the tank on course, but gradually the shore line became more distinct and before long we could see the line of houses which were our targets. Seasickness was now forgotten. It took over an hour of hard work to reach the beach and it was a miracle that most of us did. As we approached, we felt the tracks meet the shelving sand of the shore and, slowly we began to rise out of the water. We took post to deflate the screen. When the base of the screen was clear of the water, the struts were broken, the air released and the screen collapsed. We leapt into the tank and were ready for action."

"75, HE, Action – Traverse right, steady, on. 300 – white fronted house – first floor window, centre".

"On"

"Fire!"

"Within a minute of dropping our screen we had fired our first shot in anger. There was a puff of smoke and brick dust from the house we aimed at and we continued to engage our targets. Other DD tanks were coming in on both sides of us and by now we were under enemy fire from several positions, which we identified and to which we replied with 75mm and Browning machine-gun fire."

"The beach, which had been practically deserted when we arrived, was beginning to fill up fast. The infantry were wading through the surf and advancing against a hail of small arms fire and mortar bombs."

"We gave covering fire wherever we could and all the time the build-up of men and vehicles continued."

"Harry Bone's voice came over the intercom: 'Let's move up the beach a bit – I'm getting bloody wet down here!' We had landed on a fast incoming tide, so the longer we stood still the deeper the water became. As we had dropped our screen, the sea was beginning to come in over the top of the driver's hatch and by now he was sitting in a pool of water. The problem was that the promised mine clearance had not yet taken place, so we had to decide whether to press on through a known mine-field, or wait until a path had been cleared and marked."

"Suddenly, the problem was solved for us. One particularly large wave broke over the stern of the tank and swamped the engine, which spluttered to a halt. Now, with power gone, we could not move, even if we wanted to. Harry Bone and Joe Gallagher emerged from the driving compartment, soaking wet and swearing."

"More infantry were coming ashore, their small landing craft driving past us and up to the edge of the beach. There was quite a heavy fire fight in progress so we kept our guns going for as long as possible, but the water in the tank was getting deeper and we were becoming flooded. At last, we had to give up. We took out the Browning machine-guns and several cases of .3-inch belted ammunition, inflated the rubber dinghy and using the map boards as paddles began to make our way to the beach. We had not gone far when a burst of machine-gun fire hit us. Gallagher, the assistant driver, received a bullet in the ankle, the dinghy collapsed and turned over and we were all tumbled into the sea, losing our guns and ammunition. The water was quite deep and flecked with bullets all around us."

"Somehow we managed to drag Gallagher and ourselves ashore. We got clear of the water and collapsed onto the sand, soaking wet, cold and shivering. A DD tank drove up and stopped beside us with Sergeant Hepper grinning at us out of the turret. 'Can't stop!' he said, and he threw us a tin of self heating soup for which we were very grateful."

The crew eventually left the wounded Gallagher at a first aid post and, clearly being of no use to the infantry in their unarmed state, they reported their presence to the Royal Navy Beach Master who advised them to "Get off my bloody beach!" The crew made their way to the road that ran parallel to the sea, some four or five hundred yards inland and there met up with some other dismounted tank crews.

Chapter Six

Amphibious Operations After D-Day

A British DD tank photographed while taking part in the Rhine crossing. Apparently stranded at the water's edge, this vehicle may have been one of those that had difficulties with the muddy bank. Imperial War Museum photograph BU 2104

Breakout From The Bridgehead

It had been obvious from the start that crossing the rivers and water obstacles would create a great number of problems for the invading Allied force. Before the breakout from the bridgehead the three Assault Regiments RE carried out a period of training on the Orne canal, with the 5th ARRE concentrating on the handling of the 50/60-ton raft. New amphibious vehicles were becoming available.

The Terrapin was the British equivalent of the DUKW and could carry some three tons of stores on a 6-wheeled chassis. The Landing Vehicle Tracked (LVT) was an American amphibious tracked load carrier, one version of which could carry up to four tons of stores. The two types complemented each other, the Terrapin was better on hard going but found difficulty in getting out of soft mud on the river's edge, while the LVT (Buffalo) could not run any distance on hard ground because the track grousers on which it depended for propulsion when waterborne became damaged. Five Squadrons of the 1st Assault Brigade RE were trained to use these vehicles while the advance into Belgium was continuing.

Although the port of Antwerp had fallen virtually undamaged to the 11th Armoured Division early in September, it could not be used for supply purposes because the Germans controlled both banks of the Scheldt and also held the estuary.

The south bank was cleared by an attack that turned the German flank and was only made possible by the use of Buffaloes. The 2nd Canadian Corps started to clear the north bank working west from Antwerp, but encountered strong opposition on South Beveland.

To overcome this an assaulting force crossed the Scheldt in Buffaloes, supported by a Squadron of DD tanks of the Staffordshire Yeomanry to clear the opposition. Since the break-up of the 27th Armoured Brigade in Normandy the Staffordshire Yeomanry had been back to England (see appendix 'A') to convert to DD tanks under the command of the 79th Armoured Division. On their return, 'B' Squadron supported the 52nd (Lowland) Division in their South Beveland assault. This involved a swim of seven miles, which was carried out without a casualty.

The two leading flotillas set out at 02.45 hours on 25th November. Navigation and transit lights had been placed on the south bank of the Scheldt and Bofors guns firing tracer rounds provided a further check on the accuracy of the navigation on the journey that was about nine miles. The DD tanks swam ashore at 10.00 hours but their disembarkation point proved too muddy and they were diverted elsewhere. Once ashore the going was atrocious and the mud and dykes proved impassable to the Shermans, with only three tanks of this Squadron able to move inland with the infantry.

The next phase of the breakout was the capture of Walcheren, which was accomplished by a full-scale assault with LCTs following a preliminary operation by the RAF to breach the dyke at the western end of the island. Buffaloes, Crabs and AVREs were landed and gave valuable support to the Royal Marine Commandos who came ashore with them. A few days after the capture of Walcheren minesweepers started to sweep the Scheldt and Antwerp was opened for normal working on 28th November 1944.

Operation 'Veritable'

Over the winter months a series of small operations cleared the ground up to the river Maas, leaving 30 Corps poised for the attack on the Rhine. Originally planned for frozen ground, the plan had to be considerably modified now that a thaw had set in.

30 Corps, who were responsible for the operation, had first to clear the Siegfried Line, then two subsidiary lines through thickly wooded country including the Reichswald Forest and to exploit success up to the west bank of the Rhine. The ground east of Nijmegen was low lying and promised heavy going.

Operation 'Veritable' began on 8th February 1945. Crabs and AVREs opened lanes through the German minefields under conditions in which tanks became bogged and routes were only cleared with great difficulty.

The Canadians operating on the northern flank of the flooded valley of the Rhine carried out a series of amphibious attacks against the various enemy-held strongholds on the high ground that had avoided the flooding. In enemy hands these strongholds threatened the advance on the higher ground to the south.

The waterborne operations were almost full-scale naval assaults in miniature. Some were carried out in LVTs, while others involved the use of assault boats covered by the fire from the LVTs of the Assault Regiment RE and 11 RTR.

Without the LVTs it would have been impossible to clear the Germans from their strongholds.

These operations were difficult and dangerous, stray mines had been scattered over the area and the water tamped these when detonated, greatly increasing their effect.

By 9th March 1945 Operation 'Veritable' was over. It had given control of the ground up to the west bank of the river Rhine to the British and Canadian Armies. Flail Squadrons of the 79th Armoured Division working with the 9th American Army had in three days cleared minefields on their front, allowing the armour to sweep north and east across the Rhine.

Buffaloes (LVTs) during training at G Wing before the crossing the Rhine.
Photograph by kind permission of The Tank Museum

Operation 'Plunder' The Rhine Crossing

In December 1944 a new instructional wing, G Wing, opened north of Maastricht with the responsibility of working out the technique for the Rhine crossing in conjunction with HQ 12 Corps, who were in charge of the operation. At G Wing, discussion was followed by practical experiments and new equipment was devised to meet the particular conditions of this operation. This included the development of a carpet-laying Buffalo to overcome the difficulties experienced by DD tanks on soft riverbanks.

Another training wing, H Wing, was opened by the ARRE at Nijmegen on the banks of the Rhine to train Assault Squadrons in heavy rafting over a wide river. By March it had trained six Squadrons in this technique and their mastery of the class 50/60 raft proved invaluable in the early stages of the Rhine Crossing.

The last of the European wings was J Wing, devoted to navigational training. Buffaloes or DD tanks might have to work at night or in conditions of reduced

A Buffalo (LVT) crossing the river Rhine, 1945.
Photograph by kind permission of The Tank Museum

visibility due to smoke by day. Accurate direction-keeping was obviously a prime necessity if objectives were to be reached. After preliminary investigations attention was concentrated on the use of the magnetic and gyrocompasses, radio direction-keeping equipment and the use of infra-red beacons. The radio direction-keeping equipment was devised by the Division and involved the use of two type 19 sets, which, by the use of suitable ground aerials allowed tanks or Buffaloes to 'ride the beam' to their destination. DD and Buffalo Squadron commanders attended a short course in the use of these devices at the Wing, and by March 21st, G, H, and J Wings were disbanded having completed their tasks, the personnel returning to their own units.

The technique worked out by 12 Corps and the 79th Armoured Division which was based on D-Day operations was accepted by HQ Second Army who deployed two Corps for the attack, 12 Corps on the right and 30 Corps on the left. The assault was to be carried out by DD tanks and Buffaloes. Eight 50/60 rafts were to be built and since the defences were not established in great depth there was no immediate requirement for the other special equipment of the Division in the assault, although Flails, Crocodiles and AVREs were to be ferried across the river as speedily as possible in case they were required later.

The 51st (Highland) Division was to lead the advance across the Rhine, supported by the 8th Armoured Brigade, which included the DD tanks of the Staffordshire Yeomanry who had converted to DD tanks for the South Beveland operations and the 44th RTR. In preparation for the crossing the Staffordshire Yeomanry had moved to G Wing at Nijmegen and were joined on 7th March by the 44th RTR who completed just ten days training on the amphibious tanks in preparation for the Rhine crossing. The 'normal' Shermans of the latter were passed on to the 3rd County of London Yeomanry between 10th and 15th March. The 44th RTR were the only DD equipped British Regiment not to undergo any part of their DD training in the United Kingdom.

Also undergoing training at G Wing during this time was a Squadron from the 736th US Tank Battalion, which would support the American forces in their crossing of the Rhine further to the south.

A series of photographs showing men of the Staffordshire Yeomanry preparing their Sherman DD MK I tanks at G Wing. The deployment of the rope ladder for embarkation can be seen in the bottom left picture. The shell-like objects in the bottom right picture are the discarded air cylinders used to raise the flotation screen, the tank's own air cylinders being kept in reserve. By kind permission of the Staffordshire Yeomanry

At 17.00 hours on the 23rd March a tremendous air and artillery programme began. As at Nijmegen, every possible weapon took part. At 21.00 hours, the leading elements of the 51st (Highland) Division crossed in assault craft just north of Rees. They were soon followed by the DD tanks of 'C' Squadron, the Staffordshire Yeomanry, who experienced a certain amount of difficulty with mud on the far bank. The remainder of the Regiment crossed at first light and were up with the infantry before any enemy counter-attack could be launched.

The DD tanks of the Staffordshire Yeomanry were shelled in the inflation area and suffered some casualties both in men and machines. The Staffordshire Yeomanry came under enemy fire again when afloat, but despite navigational problems due to sandbanks, which it had been impossible to chart, they managed to get half a Squadron across by 05.15 hours on 24th March and had the complete Regiment across by 07.00 hours.

The 44th RTR were more fortunate than the Staffordshire Yeomanry. Their inflation was uninterrupted by enemy fire and they had no trouble while on passage, launching their first tank at 05.45 hours and, having 59 DD tanks ashore by 08.00 hours, were on their way into action with the infantry thirty minutes later.

Difficulties had been experienced on the Scheldt with muddy banks, which the tanks found difficult to climb. To overcome this G Wing had devised a chespale carpet that could be carried on the nose of a Buffalo and unrolled at will to cover an area 14 feet wide by 75 feet long. This device worked excellently and was laid by specially trained Buffalo troops at the chosen landing sites.

A Canal Defence Light (CDL) Squadron was re-formed from the 1st Tank Brigade to provide light for the crossing and the 49th RTR were pleased to take on this responsibility. They were equipped with Grant tanks mounting a CDL turret in place of their 37mm gun and were positioned on the upstream side of the areas selected for the crossing of both 12 and 30 Corps. They had three main tasks: to provide movement light, to illuminate the town of Rees to help the 1st Commando Brigade in their operations against the town and to protect the upstream flank of the assault against any waterborne assault.

The CDL tanks were extremely unpopular with the nearby infantry due to the amount of enemy fire that they attracted. On the banks of the Rhine they withstood several attacks from the air and were often engaged by hostile artillery, resulting in the loss of just one tank.

After 25th of March they were responsible for maintenance of a night watch on the river and the destruction of anything likely to sabotage the crossing places. While engaged in this role they did a considerable amount of shooting and destroyed many floating objects in the river, 35 of which exploded with a loud bang. There was much speculation that these could have been frogmen, floating mines, or perhaps even miniature submarines....

The presence of the CDL tanks almost certainly interfered with any German attempts to interrupt the crossing and the bridging operation, both of which went unimpeded.

A crowded infantry assault boat heads for the German held side of the river Rhine. Imperial War Museum photograph BU 2115

Despite the assistance of the CDL tanks the operations against the town of Rees went on for longer than was expected, with the result that bridging operations by the Royal Engineers had to be carried out while under fire from the east bank.

Tank ferries were established by the evening of 24th March and the 4th/7th Royal Dragoon Guards began to cross, followed in the next two days by the 13th/18th Hussars and the Sherwood Rangers Yeomanry. On 27th March the Brigade HQ, the 12th Battalion The King's Royal Rifle Corps and the Essex Yeomanry, who had been supporting operations from the west bank, made the crossing over the now completed class 40 bridge.

Once across the Rhine, the Second British Army were able to push forward in conjunction with operations by the American forces further south who already had a small bridgehead across the river at Remagen.

The advance continued up to and across the river Elbe, where the CDL tanks of the 79th Armoured Division were again in action, providing movement light across the river.

British infantry scramble ashore from their assault boat during the crossing of the Rhine. Imperial War Museum photograph BU 2154

Royal Engineers prepare a raft to ferry men and equipment across the Rhine during the early days of the operation. Imperial War Museum photograph BU 2131

British vehicles cross a completed class-9 bridge (9 ton maximum load) over the Rhine. Imperial War Museum photograph BU 2417

The Crossing Of The River Elbe

The crossing of the river Elbe was the last big operation of the campaign in which the DD tanks of the 79th Armoured Division took part. It was a formidable task for the river was almost as big an obstacle as the Rhine, 300 – 400 yards wide with a current running up to five knots. It had been decided that 8 Corps were to cross at Lauenberg, while 18 (US) Airborne Corps were to cross further upstream to guard the right flank of the Second British Army during their drive to capture Hamburg and reach the Baltic.

The CDL Squadron from 49th RTR who had been so useful at the Rhine crossing were brought up for the Elbe operation. It was employed to give movement light at the crossing of both the British and American troops and allowed Buffalo operations to continue throughout the hours of darkness. The ferrying operation conducted by the Buffaloes continued until a class-40 bridge had been built, and the Germans made no efforts to interrupt the crossings or to destroy the bridge.

A composite Squadron of 24 DD tanks was found from the Staffordshire Yeomanry. Despite enemy shellfire they suffered no casualties either in the inflation area or on passage. They were all on the far bank by 06.00 hours on the 30th April, an hour after they had entered the water. Until the class-40 bridge had been built they were the only armour operating on the far bank and proved themselves invaluable at both crossing places.

The small number of DD tanks available for the Elbe crossing was due to the main deficiency of the amphibious tank. The canvas flotation screen was very vulnerable to small arms fire and to shell splinters. Although this limited amount of damage could be repaired by the crew, damage caused to the extended metal deck, the air columns, or the support struts, required skilled workshop attention if the tank was to be fit to enter the water again.

A surviving 1945 Sherman DD MK III of the US Army, armed with the 76mm gun

Appendix A

War Diary of The Staffordshire Yeomanry 29th July – 25th September, 1944

29th July

Location Newhaven Harbour. Reveille 05.30 hours. Hot tea supplied to all ranks from E.S.O. Embussed for J2 Stanmere Park at 07.00 hours. Arriving there at 08.30 hours. Payparade held by Squadrons and exchange of money. Brig. Schreiber visits the Col. The Col. goes to Gosport and returns later. All personnel allowed out of camp. Casualties. Nil.

30th July

Location same. Reveille 05.30 hours. Squadrons march to Falmer station to entrain. Entrained at 09.00 hours and departed for Great Yarmouth at 09.45 hours. 'A' and 'B' Squadrons detrained at Saint Olaves for Fritton at 17.45 hours. RHQ, 'C' and HQ Squadrons detrained at Great Yarmouth at 18.15 hours. Moved into billets. 'A' and 'B' Squadrons located at W.A.W. Map Reference 67/927173.

31st July

Great Yarmouth. Reveille 07.00 hours. All personnel busy cleaning out billets and tidying up of area. At 16.00 hours muster parade for all personnel to hear farewell speech of Col Eadie. Col Pery visits the Colonel (Com. E. Nor. Sub District)

1st August

Reveille 07.00 hours. Routine as usual. A.A. and Recce. Troops attached to Squadrons for training at W.A.W. Fritton. HQ to remain in Great Yarmouth and to proceed on leave on 2nd Aug.

2nd August.

'C' Squadron and R.H.Q. Squadron proceed on seven days leave.
Routine as usual for other personnel remaining with the unit.

3rd – 10th August.

Details as for 2nd Aug.

11th August.

Reveille 07.00 hours. Routine as usual.

Leave personnel returned.

Unsuitable personnel rejoined unit and were later posted to RAC Training Depot.

12th August	Routine as usual.

12th August
Routine as usual.
'A' and 'B' Squadrons move from Fritton to Burton-on-Stather. Map reference 33/336383.

'C' Squadron move from Great Yarmouth to Fritton.
1 officer and 14 men left for France to relieve the maintenance party.

13th August
40 men unsuitable to the unit were posted to Armoured Raft Unit.

13th - 18th August
Routine as usual.

19th August
Routine as usual.
Maintenance party return from France and arrive at 06.30 hours in Newhaven and join the Regiment in great Yarmouth the same day.

20th – 23rd August
Routine as usual.

24th August
Routine as usual.
9 scout cars arrive for the Regiment from 12 A.F.V. Depot, Coventry.

'A' and 'B' Squadrons proceed on leave from Burton-on-Stather.

'C' Squadron and R.H.Q. tank troop move from Fritton to Burton-on-Stather.

25th – 27th August
Routine as usual.

28th August
Routine as usual.
60 men join the Regiment from Bovington.
Mobilisation orders received.

29th – 31st August
Routine as usual.

1st – 2nd September   Location Great Yarmouth.
Routine as usual.

3rd September   Normal Sunday Routine.
Lt Sinclair and 30 Other Ranks travelled to 19 A.F.V. Depot, Winchester to collect reinforcement tanks. Major Graham, Capt Grant, 1 W.O.II and 23 sergeants (all Canadians) attached to this unit from W.A.W.

4th September   Normal routine with packing and loading of vehicles continued on orders that this work must be completed by midnight.

Squadron leaders conference held at R.H.Q. at 14.00 hours.
Special D.Rs were sent to Cambridge to collect movement orders.

Movement orders received in the evening and the road party are to leave as soon as possible the following day.

5th September   The road party set off at approx. 10.00 hours and proceeded under command of Major Gardner to Stevenage, via Newmarket. They were accommodated at Stevenage Transit Camp for the night. A hot meal was served on arrival.
The remainder of personnel remained at Yarmouth and are to travel by train on 6th September.

6th September   The train party arrived at A.18 camp (about 6 miles from Gosport) and the road party joined them later in the day, after a good run from Stevenage via Watford and North London suburbs then Aldershot and Parnham to A.18.

On arrival at A.18 personnel had a hot meal and accommodation was found for them in tents, except for vehicle drivers who slept in their vehicles, as vehicles were parked on side of the main road.

The Tank Party from Winchester and Fritton arrived on transporters at Transit Camp A.19 near Gosport.

7th September

All personnel except the Tank Party remained at A.18 for the whole day but were allowed out in the evening. During the day 24-hour ration packs were issued along with emergency rations and other equipment required for a sea journey.
The tanks remained at A.19.

8th September

All personnel left A.18 during the morning at convenient intervals and proceeded to the outskirts of Gosport where they embarked on one or other of two L.S.Ts which as soon as loaded drew out into deep water at approx. 16.00 hours. Good meals were served whilst on board and the majority of personnel were accommodated in bunks but a few had to sleep on deck with their vehicles.

The tanks moved early to the hards at Gosport but after waiting all day were still not loaded at night and at 20.30 hours moved to Camp A.16 (north of Fareham for the night).

9th September

The L.S.Ts drew against piers at approx. 14.00 hours after an uneventful and calm crossing. On disembarking all personnel and vehicles preceded to 60 Transit Camp, where parties reformed. Food was provided and some personnel slept in tents but the majority of the road party remained with their vehicles on the parking ground.

The tanks and party left A.16 at first light and about midday started to load on the L.C.T.(4)s. Three transporters and tanks and one 3-tonner of R.A.S.C. on each L.C.T. transporters were loaded on the craft with considerable difficulty by D.8. tractors.

The first wave of L.C.Ts. left for France at 23.00 hours.

19th September New routine as follows

Reveille	06.15 hours
Roll Call	06.30 hours
Sick Parade	07.00 hours
Breakfast	07.15 hours
Parade	08.00 hours
Dinner	13.00 hours
Parade	14.00 – 17.00 hours
Tea	17.30 hours
Guard Mounting	18.30 hours

A special maintenance programme was put into effect.

NAAFI rations of approx 100 cigarettes per man plus chocolates, razor blades and other commodities were sold in the Regt.

22nd September Captured German rations were issued to the men, although of good quality they did not prove very popular.

23rd September 'C' Squadron 'dipped' their tanks in the Lido adjacent H.Q.

Squadron area early in the morning and the results proved satisfactory.

Half-day holiday after 13.00 hours, when Regimental transport was arranged to convey personnel to Brussels.

A further cinema show was given to the unit and more German rations were issued.

24th September Normal working day until 13.00 hours.

A Church of England Service was held in the recreation room. A Roman Catholic service was attended by members of the Regiment in Elewyt Parish Church. 'A' Squadron dipped their tanks early in the morning and the results proved to be satisfactory. First mail arrived at the unit since leaving England.

25th September   Normal routine except for 'B' Squadron who left camp before 06.00 hours to 'dip' their tanks in the Lido. They returned to camp at approx. 08.15 hours. The results were as satisfactory as for the other two Squadrons.

Bibliography

"A Trooper's Desert War", Philip Foster

"British and American Tanks of World War Two", Peter Chamberlain and Chris Ellis, Cassel and Co.

"By Tank into Normandy", by Stuart Hills, 2002

"D-Day", by Richard Collier, Cassell, 1992

"Extracts From The Diary of Lt Col S D Christopherson DSO, MC," Squadron Leader, 'A' Squadron as Major Christopherson

"Final Flights", Ian McLachlan, Haynes

"Forrard", The Story of The East Riding Yeomanry, Paul Mace, 2001

"History of The 13th/18th Royal Hussars (Queen Mary's Own) 1922 – 1947", by Major-General Charles H Miller

"Move Out-Verify, Combat Story of The 743rd Tank Battalion", 1945

"Normandy 1944 From The Hull of a Sherman", Arthur Reddish

"Regimental History of The 4th/7th Royal Dragoon Guards",

"Regimental History of The East Riding Yeomanry",

"Sherman Fire-Fly", Mark Bill Hayward, 2002

"Strike Swiftly", Marvin Jenson, 1997

"The 79th Armoured Division", N W Duncan, Profile Publications Limited

"The Universal Tank", David Fletcher

"Wheels & Tracks", *Issue Number 40*

"Young Man In A Tank", by Group Captain RAF (Retired) Patrick Hennessey MBE

Terms and Abbreviations

ARK   Bridge laying tank

ATEA   Amphibious Tank Escape Apparatus

AVRE   Assault Vehicle Royal Engineers

BARV   Beach Armoured Recovery Vehicle

BIGOT   Any allied officer who knew the location of the planned D-Day landings

CDL   Canal Defence Searchlight tank

COPPs   Combined Operations Pilotage Parties

Crab   Mine clearance tank equipped with rotating chain flails

Crocodile   Churchill tank equipped with flame thrower in place of bow machine gun

D-Day   'Day Day', Normandy Landings 4th June 1944

DD   Duplex Drive Amphibious Tank

DSEA   Davis Submerged Escape Apparatus

LCT   Landing Craft Tank

LCA   Landing Craft Assault

LCN   Landing Craft Navigation (modified LCA)

LST   Landing Ship Tank

LVT   Landing Vehicle Tank (Buffalo)

Index

79th Armoured Division — *6, 8, 10, 11, 12, 14, 15, 31, 34, 47, 58, 60, 86, 107, 109, 111, 15, 117, 125*

Amphibious Tank Escape Apparatus — *44, 63, 73, 126*

Ark — *13, 126*

Assault Vehicle Royal Engineers — *11, 12, 13, 66, 72, 77, 98, 103, 108, 111*

Bay of Naples — *89*

Beach Armoured Recovery Vehicle — *100, 126*

Bernieres-sur-mer — *101*

Bigot — *90, 126*

Bradley — *8, 66, 90*

Buffalo (LVT) — *107, 108, 110, 111, 113, 117, 126*

Canal Defence Searchlight Tank — *11, 14, 56, 69, 113, 114, 115, 117, 126*

Clogstoun-Willmott — *94*

Combined Operations — *41, 86, 94, 126*

Courselles-sur-mer — *101*

Crab — *14, 15, 108*

Crocodile — *15, 68, 72, 77, 111, 126*

Cyril Hutton — *35, 36*

Davis Submerged Escape Apparatus — *43, 44, 62, 73, 80, 126*

D-Day
- Gold Beach — *92, 96, 98*
- Juno Beach — *86, 101*
- Omaha Beach — *95, 96, 98*
- Sword Beach — *92, 102, 103*
- Utah Beach — *92, 94*

DD Equipped Formations

- 3rd Hussars	*37*
- 4th/7th Royal Dragoon Guards	*22, 60, 72, 74, 78, 81, 85, 86, 92, 93, 96, 115, 125*
- 6th Canadian Armoured Regt. (1st Hussars)	*56, 86, 87 93, 10,*
- 7th Hussars	*37*
- 10th Canadian Armoured Regt. (Fort Garry Horse)	*56, 70, 86, 87, 93, 101*
- 13th/18th Hussars	*58, 59, 71, 93, 102, 115*
- 27th Armoured Brigade	*12, 14, 56, 60, 78, 85, 86, 93, 107*
- 70th US Tank Battalion	*56, 88, 89, 92, 93*
- 191st US Tank Battalion	*89*
- 741st US Tank Battalion	*22, 56, 88, 93, 95*
- 743rd US Tank Battalion	*22, 56, 88, 93, 96, 125*
- 753rd US Tank Battalion	*89*
- 756th US Tank Battalion	*89*
- East Riding Yeomanry	*31, 47, 60, 78, 79, 125*
- Nottinghamshire Yeomanry (Sherwood Rangers)	*3, 22, 81, 85, 86, 92, 93, 98, 115*
- Staffordshire Yeomanry	*3, 5, 85, 86, 107, 111, 113, 117, 119*
Dieppe	*10, 12, 17, 59*
Duplex Drive	*6, 11, 12, 16, 17, 25, 29, 32, 58, 87, 92, 126*
Exercise Smash I	*73*
Flotation Screen	*6, 19, 22, 27, 30, 35, 36, 41, 47 49, 67, 75, 76, 117*

Fritton Lake

    - Fatal Training Accident   *See Trooper Lloyd*

    - Mock-Up Landing Craft Ramp   *34, 40, 78*

    - B17 Flying Fortress Crash   *46, 50*

    - P47 Thunderbolt Crash   *49*

    - DD Training   *See 'Training Wing A'*

Gosport   *62, 63, 64, 66, 69, 70, 75, 87, 88, 101, 119, 121, 122*

Great Yarmouth   *62, 72, 78, 82, 84, 87, 88, 89, 119, 120, 121*

Gyro-Compass   *25*

Infra-Red Beacon   *94, 111*

Italy   *37*

Hobart   *8, 11, 12, 58, 66, 73*

Houlgate   *102*

Invergordon   *68*

Landing Craft Tank   *56, 68, 126*

Landing Craft Assault   *96, 97, 126*

Landing Craft Navigation   *I94, 126*

Landing Ship Tank   *90, 126*

Landing Vehicle Tank   *See Buffalo*

Le Havre   *102*

Le Hamel   *99*

Lion-sur-mer   *72*

Lowestoft   *6, 50, 79*

Lowestoft Swimming Baths   *73, 79*

Montgomery   *69, 75, 90*

Moray Firth   *66, 67, 68, 75, 80*

Nijmegen   *108, 110, 111, 113*

Operation Overlord   *72, 86*

Operation Plunder   *110*

Operation Tiger   *89, 90*

Operation Veritable   *108, 109*

Orford Ness   *65, 69*

Propellers   *25, 29, 60, 69, 89, 103*

Rendlesham Hall   *78*

River Crossings

    - Elbe   *8, 94, 115, 117*

    - Maas   *108*

    - Orne   *102, 107*

    - Po   *37*

    - Rhine   *8, 37, 89, 94, 108, 109, 110, 111, 113, 115, 117*

    - Scheldt   *107, 108, 113*

St. Aubin-sur-mer   *101*

Saint Olaves   *49, 119*

Salerno   *89*

Sherman DD   *6, 19, 22, 25, 27, 28, 29, 34, 35, 36, 37, 48, 49, 69, 77, 81, 84, 85, 87, 88, 89, 95, 96, 98, 101*

Slapton Sands   *89, 90*

Steering Tiller   *25, 61*

Studland Bay   *37, 73, 75*

Tetrarch   *19*

Training

    - Wing A   *45*

    - Wing G   *110, 111, 113*

    - Wing H   *110*

    - Wing J   *110, 111*

Trooper Lloyd   *47, 79*

Valentine DD   *6, 17, 19, 25, 34, 35, 37, 47, 49, 62, 75, 77, 78, 79, 87, 89*

Ver-sur-mer   *98*

Whatmough   *36, 37*

Woodbridge   *60, 64, 65*